"Luke Norsworthy's inviting, accessible, and entirely enjoyable new book is an invitation to come to know God better. Or to come to know God for the first time. Highly recommended."

James Martin, SJ, author of *Jesus: A Pilgrimage* and *The Jesuit Guide*

"Luke's insight and humor come through his stories and theology in beautifully carved pieces we can savor long after the reading is over. Part memoir, part preaching, part amazing storytelling—it's all a gift offered by a man of great faith who has chosen God over everything. Luke is an exceptional podcaster, pastor, writer, and friend. Read his book."

Becca Stevens, author, priest, and founder of Thistle Farms

"What a generous gift! Norsworthy opens wide the door of his heart to reveal his struggle to find a path through the dark woods of spiritual doubt and uncertainty. This book is alternately moving and humorous, and Luke doesn't abandon us in the now-all-too-familiar landscape of religious cynicism but instead joyfully leads us into the land of hope and resurrection."

Ian Morgan Cron, author of *The Road Back to You*; host of the podcast *Typology*

"*God over Good*, by turns hilarious and heartbreaking, is the urgent, raw, and honest story of a pastor who almost lost his faith. Luke Norsworthy challenges us—the cynics and the skeptics alike—to find God beyond our expectations. Blessed, indeed, are those who leap."

Richard Beck, author of *Unclean*, *Reviving Old Scratch*, and *Stranger God*

"Luke does such a brave job in this book—telling the truth, asking the questions many of us aren't willing to ask (but hear in our heads), and walking us all toward honesty and freedom and the person we really want to be. *God over Good* will rescue you in ways you didn't know you needed rescuing. That's what it did for me too. I'm forever grateful."

Annie F. Downs, bestselling author of *100 Days to Brave* and *Looking for Lovely*

"Despite all the chiding that they just need to have faith, that doubt needs to be doubted, and that they can abound in confidence, many believers still struggle with uncertainty. But thankfully that does not mean they don't belong among the faithful! In this debut book—less apologetics and more a collection of stories of faith—Norsworthy points such people toward those resources where fresh courage and risky faith for the long journey are formed—resources such as Scripture, the community of believers, and ultimately, the risen Christ. One of the highest compliments I can offer is true about this work: it is spiritually honest!"

Mike Cope, director of ministry outreach, Pepperdine University

"Beneath the gentle humor of this book, there is a serious wrestling with a most profound truth. Any faith worth having cannot be with a god of our wishes but only with the God who authentically meets us in Jesus, Scripture, life, and suffering. As Luke shows, this means we must give up much of what we expected, but oh, what we gain!"

Randy Harris, professor of Bible, missions, and ministry, Abilene Christian University

"This is the Luke I've come to know and love as a friend and fellow pastor—refreshingly honest, exceedingly bright, and unapologetically faithful. *God over Good* is an indispensable companion for anyone wrestling with a faith that doesn't fit their old categories but who hopes to discover that God is with them in their spiritual evolution."

Jason Adam Miller, founder and lead pastor of South Bend City Church

"Luke transparently shares the struggle many have with a faith focused on certain answer because that type of faith ends up delivering only more questions. But Luke doesn't leave us there; he shows us a way to the other side of cynicism. God isn't what we always expect, but God is always beautiful. There is life and love on the other side of simplicity, and Luke guides us toward it."

Fr. Richard Rohr, author of *Everything Belongs* and *Falling Upward*

"In *God over Good*, Luke Norsworthy writes with pastoral concern and personal candor as he insightfully and often humorously navigates the challenges to a sustained Christian faith. Norsworthy helps us understand that what may initially threaten our faith can actually become the catalyst to a far deeper and richer faith. As Norsworthy points out, 'This death, burial, and resurrection isn't just an event but a lifestyle.'"

Brian Zahnd, lead pastor of Word of Life Church, St. Joseph, Missouri; author of *Sinners in the Hands of a Loving God*

GOD
OVER
GOOD

GOD
OVER
GOOD

SAVING YOUR FAITH
BY LOSING YOUR
EXPECTATIONS OF GOD

LUKE NORSWORTHY

BakerBooks
a division of Baker Publishing Group
Grand Rapids, Michigan

© 2018 by Luke Norsworthy

Published by Baker Books
a division of Baker Publishing Group
PO Box 6287, Grand Rapids, MI 49516-6287
www.bakerbooks.com

Printed in the United States of America

Library of Congress Cataloging-in-Publication Data
Names: Norsworthy, Luke, 1981– author.
Title: God over good : saving your faith by losing your expectations of God / Luke Norsworthy.
Description: Grand Rapids : Baker Publishing Group, 2018. | Includes bibliographical references.
Identifiers: LCCN 2018009830 | ISBN 9780801093326 (cloth)
Subjects: LCSH: Faith. | God (Christianity) | Expectation (Psychology)—Religious aspects—Christianity.
Classification: LCC BV4637 .N67 2018 | DDC 231.7—dc23
LC record available at https://lccn.loc.gov/2018009830

To protect the privacy of those who have shared their stories with the author, some details and names have been changed.

Published in association with the literary agency of Daniel Literary Group, LLC, Brentwood, TN.

18   19   20   21   22   23   24   7   6   5   4   3   2   1

To those who most truly display goodness to me,

my girls.

Be merciful to those who doubt.

Jude 22 NIV

CONTENTS

ANTS

Let's go ahead and make this awkward.

You've driven deep into the woods with two living creatures in the backseat of your car that you are going to set free in the wild.

The emancipation begins when you unbuckle a tiny ant from its tiny car seat, which you fashioned from Monopoly game pieces and duct tape. You carry him on your index finger down to a nice mound of dirt, and off he scurries into the woods.

The second creature to be freed into the wild is a baby. As in a baby human.

The ant looks quite . . . antish, you know, tiny with a thin, crusty shell. Probably just a few months old. The baby human is squishy and loud, also a few months old.

After you've dropped off the ant and the baby in the forest and driven back home, which one has a better shot of surviving in the woods alone?

The ant could find a colony to join, where it could live a productive life of digging holes and carrying items weighing twenty times its body weight.

The likelihood of the baby growing up is not as strong. To be fair, babies have survived in the woods alone before—obviously, that's how we got Tarzan. So there's historical evidence that it could happen.

Still, if you are a betting person, you are going to put your money on the ant's survival. And just so we are all on the same page, the least degenerate part of this scenario until now is the gambling.

Why does an ant that resides at the bottom of the food chain have a higher survival rate than the human, the creature at the top of the food chain?

An exoskeleton.

The ant has zero vertebrae; instead, it has an exoskeleton—its thin, crusty shell—which creates a defense against the world. The exoskeleton almost instantly gives the ant a high survival rate, but it also inhibits the ant from ascending to higher levels of growth. The ant remains at its safe starting point forever.

A human baby is extremely vulnerable, but if you give him twenty years, he will have the strength and the intelligence—not to mention control over his opposable thumbs—to be the most powerful creature on the earth, assuming he doesn't waste his days staring at a phone. The human's thirty-three vertebrae create his endoskeleton, which gives him a core to build around, not a shell to be encased in.

If you want a higher probability of surviving the first year alone in the forest, you would choose the exoskeleton.

If you want to thrive for a century, you would choose not outward protection but sustainability that comes from the inside.

What gives the initial feeling of a safe start can become the limitation that prevents ascension to higher levels of maturity.

For some, faith begins with a hard shell, a rigid set of answers and platitudes that keep them safe but eventually prevent them from growing into who they could be. The system that was initially protecting them now traps them.

You and I have just proven we are able to get through a metaphor described by my wife (and the mother of my three babies) as "demented" and by my agent as "creepy."

I promise the book gets less creepy from here.

I also promise that if you've ever felt trapped by a system of understanding God that got you started safely but is now preventing you from growing, it's possible to let go of the expectations that made you feel safe so that you can develop a life-giving core. You don't need to let go of God; you only need to let go of your expectations.

But the transformation isn't easy.

At least it wasn't for me.

1

Can't Sing

The worshipers' energy fills the spacious room as everyone sings without restraint.

Everyone except me.

A thousand voices fill the sanctuary with full-throated declarations of trust in God's deliverance and salvation, while I can't muster a squeak from my paralyzed voice box. It's not that I don't know how to sing. I've never been confused for Sinatra or Timberlake, but I grew up singing in church with no instruments, just voices. We broke into four-part harmonies of "Happy Birthday" at birthday parties.

I've been singing my entire life, but not this day, because during every declaration of faith sung, I silently doubt.

They all sing, "You're a good, good Father."

I literally have a good, good father named Larry. He's an A+ father, and he doesn't act the way our heavenly parent acts. I know my dad; I know how he thinks and how he acts. If I want to see him, he makes time for me. If I call him, he almost always answers his phone. If I text him, he answers, often signing off his texts with "Love, Dad" just to make sure I know the text was from him. I don't have doubts about the existence of Larry or his desire to be in relationship with me, but I do about my heavenly parent.

My good, good father, Larry, has gone to great lengths to prevent suffering for me. And if Larry became all powerful, I'm sure he would completely eradicate suffering in my life. But that's not what the all-powerful heavenly parent has done.

God makes suffering easy to know, but God's identity often seems like a mystery. So of course I'm not singing, "You're a good, good Father," because that's not how I define what a good, good parent is.

It didn't used to be like this. I used to be the hands-raised, heart-abandoned type in the front row, like an adoring tween at a boy band concert.

If the Bible said it, I believed it. If something happened, I confidently knew it was part of God's plan, and I didn't need to worry, because God doesn't make mistakes.

And everything made sense to me. Any question had an answer; I just had to be willing to look hard enough to find it. Any issue had a corresponding Bible verse that would clear everything up. Any mystery could be illuminated with the right sermon or the right book. So I invested in this pursuit. I didn't just dabble in religion on the weekends. I moved all my chips to the center of the table with no hedging. I was so deep in the game that I even had a Jesus fish on the back of my car.

Now, not only am I losing the faith I grew up singing about, but I'm also losing my vocation.

Cracking

I'm a pastor.

Twenty years ago I went off to college as a sixteen-year-old with God and the academic system figured out. I preached my first sermon the next year as a sophomore in college. By my junior year, I was preaching every Sunday in the tiny West Texas town of Moran, population 211. In that old, wooden church building, I made cocksure declarations about who God is and how God works, while the cockfighting roosters raised next door made their own declarations.

The next year I earned my undergraduate degree in Christian ministry and began seminary to earn a degree pompously titled Master of Divinity, because of course you can master the divine in a few short years in graduate school.

Altogether I've worked at half a dozen churches, including the church I started when I was twenty-six. Now I'm wondering about my foundation's sturdiness as my sandcastle of certainty is cracking.

The first sign of water breaking through happened after I completed the final in my Introduction to Old Testament class. Up until that moment, I was convinced I had a firm grip on God and the Bible. I had built a structure to make sense of the world—or maybe, more honestly, to make my world small enough that I could master it. After I finished the final exam, a tiny crack opened in my soul, and out leaked the first little bit of certainty. In that class I saw the Old Testament's flippant lack of concern for what I needed the Old Testament to be. I wanted my sacred text to be above criticism. I wanted it to match every scientific and historical account. I wanted the God it described to be one who made faith easy. I wanted my faith to be without contradiction or complication, and my sacred text wasn't doing its part. I get that my request for three-thousand-year-old literature to match my modern expectations is a bit much, but is it too much for God to avoid commanding his people to commit genocide?

And if I couldn't rely on the Old Testament to be what I needed it to be, how much more of the Bible could I trust?

The crack in my faith began with intellectual inconsistencies, but my struggle didn't remain ideological. My struggle wasn't just about the terrifying Old Testament texts in which God commanded entire people groups to be killed or the contradictory accounts of events or the Bible's overall inability to stay in the lines I had drawn for it. It was also about my experiences.

It was my mom's chronic illness that never got better.

It was my brother's divorce, despite all my prayers to stop it.

It was the train wreck of my first full-time ministry job after seminary.

It was the church plant that never grew into what I dreamed for it to be.

It was that moment from my childhood I had always kept at bay that eventually resurfaced.

If the choice is to sit in the fetal position crying or to suppress emotions so you can keep on moving, sometimes you've just got to push the emotions down. But they will not stay down there forever. They will eventually come up, just like the story of the five-year-old girl from my childhood. It stayed buried deep down until I had a five-year-old daughter.

Feelings Resurfacing

As a kid, I lived just outside Philadelphia, a few miles from historic Valley Forge Park. My parents built our home on a densely wooded plot. And by "my parents built," I mean they literally did most of the manual labor, from framing the walls to hanging the green wallpaper in the kitchen to getting our front door and staircase rail from a nearby Amish family. Our entire upstairs was just subfloor and studs when we first moved in. When it was time for my brother and me to get our own rooms, my dad had to build walls and lay carpet in an unfinished room. If my parents had done this thirty years later, they could have been on some weird home-remodel reality TV show.

Twenty yards behind our DIY home, the backyard dropped precipitously for about a hundred yards. At the bottom of the hill was a twisty road hidden underneath the canopy of tree branches. Just beyond the road was a creek with bugs, rocks, and the occasional snake—an ideal place for kids to play. The marked speed for the road was forty-five miles per hour, which, along with the trees lining the road and the curves in the road, reduced visibility for drivers to next to nothing.

As a five-year-old, I was playing behind my house with two sisters who were family friends, one my age and the other just a few years older. The girls heard the sound of the creek and couldn't resist the temptation to go play in the water. I knew that going down to the creek unsupervised was against the rules, but we decided to do it anyway.

Standing on the dirt just off the shoulder of the road, we hatched a plan for traversing the road: we would cross one at a time by birth order.

The older sister went across the curvy road first. She stood on the other side of the road and waved back.

Next up, the younger sister.

Just then, around the corner came a Ford Bronco driven by a nurse coming home from work. Between the height of the vehicle, the trees, the bend in the road, and the assigned speed, the nurse had no way of seeing the little girl who was on the street directly in front of her vehicle.

And no one from above intervened to save her.

Three decades later I recall two scenes from that day. The first scene took place back up the hill in our kitchen with the green wallpaper as I called 911.

The second scene involved red, flashing lights of the first-responder vehicles covering our front yard as workers tried to keep the little girl alive.

The girl survived, but her brain, her body, and her family were never the same.

This story sat in the recesses of my brain for decades like a dust-covered book in the back of a library until my oldest daughter was the same age as that little girl. I couldn't imagine singing about God being a good Father if God didn't rescue my little girl when she tried to cross the road.

I've had wonderfully positive experiences too, of course, but it's not like forty-seven negative experiences are balanced out by forty-seven positive, grace-filled experiences. Unlike joy, suffering doesn't add. Suffering multiplies.

Suffering is historical.

Suffering recalls previous heartbreaks, intellectual and experiential, to compound with the present moment's worries.

Which is why, years later, I stand surrounded by a thousand people singing songs about God being a good Father, and my faith has gone mute.

Doubting

A few months after my singing predicament, I was in a North Hollywood apartment for a podcast interview. I'd barely gotten into my normal, introductory, awkward attempts at humor when that episode's guest, agnostic comedian Brent Sullivan, interjected, "Do you know any pastors who doubt?"

I was dumbfounded. Podcast guests don't ask questions. And if they do, they never ask questions that personal. I was sure Brent didn't mean his question to be personal. How could he know it would be so intrusive?

He didn't know that the entire reason I had started my podcast and recorded hundreds of episodes was to get respected people to help me make sense of the faith I was fighting to keep. He didn't know I had been pulled out of my certainty into the unknown and was drowning in my disorientation, desperately looking for deliverance. I had given up on a lifeboat; I just hoped for a piece of driftwood to keep me temporarily afloat.

"Do you know any pastors who doubt?"

"Um . . ."

The truthful answer was simple and straightforward. I just didn't want to say it. "Yes, I know a pastor who doubts. I see him every morning in the mirror."

I remained silent, but my thoughts did not. Should I bury this tension, disregarding what doing so will do to my soul? That's assuming I, in fact, have a soul. This "sweep it under the rug" approach comes naturally to me. But I've become self-aware enough to know that, like a dirty diaper hidden in the back of a closet, the junk I try to bury in my soul gets progressively worse the longer it's unattended.

So if I step into the mystery and end up losing my faith entirely, what am I going to do for a job?

I could just go through the motions, because pastoring is the only way I know to make a living. I have a few decades before I retire, so this wouldn't be quick or easy, but I have three daughters to support. Luckily, there are always sermons on iTunes to be borrowed.

Maybe I just need to try harder to rebuild the wall I once safely stood behind. If I retrace my steps, the ones I took when my faith was good, then maybe my old faith will be resurrected. Sure, I've tried this multiple times before with no success, but this just might be the time I can switch on the good old Luke.

I remember the good old Luke, the one back in college.

A decade into marriage, my wife told me that when we were first dating in college, she had a tough time not confusing me for Jesus. But now, and I quote, "Luke, I don't have that problem anymore."

To be fair, I did have longer hair back then.

But maybe if I retrace the steps, read the same verses, and pray the same way, I can become more like the easy-to-confuse-for-Jesus Luke again. Maybe I should just keep shoveling the same sand into the same cracks in the same wall in hopes that somehow the water will finally stop getting in.

Or maybe there's another way.

Maybe salvation isn't about trying to get back behind the wall of certainty and confidence.

Maybe salvation isn't about trying to force God to match my expectations for what God should be.

Maybe salvation isn't about running from my doubts as though they are the enemy of my relationship with God but instead embracing them as the very place where I meet God.

Maybe salvation looks more like letting go than holding on.

Building the Wall

When I was twelve years old, our family moved to rural southeast Ohio. I brought my Philadelphia swagger and two fake front teeth, courtesy of one little fight on the playground, the same playground where I spent most of my days.

And yes, I did get those front teeth around Christmastime, forever ruining that stupid Christmas song.

Fast-forward a few more years, and I'm a fifteen-year-old on a date with a girl I really like. On my back porch, I've set up a picturesque dinner of peanut butter and jelly sandwiches, because I've always been a romantic.

While in the midst of asking this young lady if she is tired, because she's been running through my mind all day, I bite into my sandwich, and a peculiar and painfully cool breeze rushes into my mouth.

Why my mouth was open wide enough to notice a cool breeze while chewing on food is another story.

My tongue slides to the front of my mouth to assess the situation and finds an unexpected opening at the location where one of my front teeth used to be. I panic.

In an attempt to fully ascertain the situation, I clear my mouth by swallowing the current contents, which I instantaneously know to be a mistake. I don't care how charming you are. When your front tooth falls out on a date and then you swallow it, the date is over.

After the date's unceremonious conclusion, I'm whisked away to a far less romantic place, the dentist office, to get a new front tooth. The dentist wants both of my front teeth to match, so he also replaces the faithful old fake front tooth that didn't abandon me during my time of great need. Kind of like when one of the tires on your car has a blowout, but instead of getting just one replacement, you get a completely new set of tires.

But unlike with tires, one doesn't get a permanent tooth in a day. The process to make teeth that fit your specific mouth takes weeks. So in the meantime, you get temporary teeth. Which fit your mouth about as well as a spare tire that's road tested for only fifty miles per hour fits your car.

A temporary tooth isn't given the craftsmanship of a permanent tooth, at least my temporary teeth weren't. They were okay to be there, but we all knew they didn't really belong. It's kind of like how you would feel if you were in a library and ran into one of the Kardashians. It's okay for them to be there, but we all know they don't really belong.

So I go to summer camp that week with substandard fake teeth. And luckily, kids are not mean.

Correction: kids are actually the meanest creatures on earth.

Another camper, a pretty, black-haired pastor's daughter, is doing crafts with me when she notices a similarity between my temporary front teeth and the gum she is chewing.

"Luke, your teeth look like someone shoved two pieces of Chiclets gum in your mouth," the tweenage antichrist says.

In an instant, I am no longer Luke. I am now known as Chiclets to my fellow campers, all because of the pastor's daughter with hair as dark as her soul.

And that is all I hear throughout the entire day.

Chiclets.

Chiclets.

Chiclets.

But the story doesn't end in art class with our hero being verbally assaulted by the pastor's daughter. That afternoon our villain is playing softball. As she is about to field a ground ball at third base, the ball takes a funny bounce off the infield. Some people call what happened to that ball a "bad hop."

I'm not one of them.

The ball bounces up above her glove, hitting her directly in the mouth, reminiscent of the smooth stone flying out of David's sling and striking the evil villain Goliath.

And the pretty villain's front tooth is never the same again. It is now broken just like mine.

That is the day I start believing in God.

Well, technically, this isn't exactly how I began my relationship with God. It began a few months before, but the story I just told is much better than my actual story.

Turning toward God

My deeply devoted parents and grandparents raised me in a conservative religious environment. As a ten-year-old, I was baptized because I wanted to follow Jesus like my parents and partly to get the refreshments that were passed during the service, aka the Eucharist, that were off-limits for the nonbaptized.

After my baptism, I continued to act like a normal kid, exploring boundaries and experimenting with the major sins all youth pastors preach against: drinking beer and listening to rap music.

My baptism, as it is for many raised in a religious community, was a rite of passage more than a drastic Saul of Tarsus type conversion. The turn in my life happened in the tenth grade when I started daily Bible reading. I still can't place why I began reading the Bible every day, but I did.

I've always been very grounded in routine, so part of this new practice's staying power was due to my predisposition to habit, but it was also because of my dad's participation. My psychologist dad, upon noticing my Bible reading, began subtly reinforcing the behavior. It wouldn't surprise me to find out that he rewarded me by clandestinely placing sugar cubes in my cereal after my morning Bible reading. He might have even used an elaborate Pavlovian bell system to subconsciously cue me to go read. But the only reinforcements I can recall were the subtle inquiries about that day's reading. I assume the rest of his reinforcements are buried deep in my subconscious.

"Luke, what did you read today?"

"I read Romans 3, 4, and 5."

"Oh, that's great, Luke."

That's all it was, but also all I needed.

I religiously read the Bible without fail, and I was changed in a profound way. The boundary exploration ceased. I even discarded my hidden collection of "Parental Advisory: Explicit Lyrics" CDs.

The God I read about in the Bible gave me order and direction for life. I found something I could use to calibrate my existence. I wanted straightforward answers that would tell me the appropriate actions to take and the right way to live. And that's what I found in my newfound faith.

The Great Debate

A year into this new phase, I participated in my first debate over the legitimacy of Christianity. Mike, an atheist on my high school wrestling team, brought up a question over lunch in the cafeteria. Which then became a conversation in the locker room, which led to even more discussions on the wrestling mats after practice. And then the debate continued into the next day, the next week, the next month.

The conversations were cordial and positive, but incessant. Mike would often show up to school with printouts of critiques of Christianity he had found online. The internet was a different world back then, as Al Gore had just barely given birth to it. There wasn't a great wealth of resources for Mike to glean from, so Mike's questions were the intro to biblical criticism type questions that were advanced for a teenager but not that troubling for many students of Scripture.

> How can the Bible be true if Matthew, Mark, Luke, and John disagree on the order of events in Jesus's life?
>
> Why do the stories in the Old Testament, including the two creation stories in Genesis, contradict each other?

Before the school year ended, we declared a truce. The debates ceased, with neither of us making any concessions to the other's side. We continued to be friends but didn't interact much, as I was going off to college and Mike was still in high school. That next fall Mike surprised me with a call to my college dorm room to inform me he was converting from atheism to Christianity. My grandfather baptized Mike soon after the call.

But Mike wasn't the only one converted in those conversations.

The debating during the early part of my faith led me on a path of intellectualizing my faith into a sturdy wall built to withstand attacks on my beliefs. I continued to read apologetics books and rehearse arguments against would-be critics in an effort to build an impenetrable case against external attacks or my own internal doubts. I studied diligently partly because I didn't like to lose at anything, whether it be sports or a debate about religion. My embryonic faith was poured into that same immature me versus them competitive mold, causing faith to become an argument to be mastered instead of a relationship to be cherished. I read the Bible to know my talking points, not to know my Creator.

Another friend from my teenage years showed up at our church after moving across the country to live with his aunt and uncle. Upon going to his house for the first time, I was shocked by his bedroom's cleanliness. My parents made me clean my room, but they didn't require me to have a closet that looked like an IKEA commercial like his. Every subsequent time I went to his house, his room was just as immaculate.

And it wasn't clean because he was forced to clean it by his aunt and uncle. It didn't make sense to me at the time why a thirteen-year-old would always have such a tidy room. But it makes some sense to me now.

My friend had moved to live with his aunt and uncle because his mother had tragically passed away in a car accident. If that had happened to me, I can't imagine how out of control I would have felt being a teenager who, in an instant, had lost his friends, his school, his house, and most of all, his mom. Years later I wonder if the reason he kept his room so pristine was because it was the only thing he could control. He couldn't control where he lived, whom he lived with, or the school he attended, but he could control how well his bed was made, how vacuumed his floor was, and how straight his closet was. He was controlling the only things he could.

I approached understanding God this same way. I wanted to control something, but for all my efforts to overcome any mess, I couldn't keep my faith completely clean. One question would get answered, but then another question would emerge. I felt as if I were fighting a leaky wall, putting a finger in one hole to stop the water from coming in only to discover that the water had found another crack to leak through.

I thought I was just another book, another sermon, another degree away from having a perfectly built wall, but I was wrong, because you can't get unknowing all the way down to zero.

The New Questions

I wish I could go back to the questions Mike asked me in high school. I wish my biggest concern was the inability to reconcile biblical stories with each other or to reconcile science and faith. I'm two decades removed from the high school cafeteria inquisition, and my question now isn't any of the ones covered in intro to biblical interpretation. Now I wonder if the biblical stories should even be read because the Bible isn't the good, sacred text I want it to be.

Prominent Jewish stories aren't as unique as I want them to be. The very first story in the Bible, the first creation account in Genesis, sounds quite similar to the *Enuma Elish*, the creation account of the Babylonians, who were the Jews' neighbors. Both the *Enuma Elish* and the first creation account in Genesis have matter existing before creation, which is ordered by the divine. Both have darkness preceding creation and light existing before the creation of the sun, moon, and stars. In the *Enuma Elish*, the goddess Tiamat personifies the sea, while in Genesis, the word for the water (*deep*) in Hebrew is the word *tehom*, which many believe to be a derivative of Tiamat. The orders of creation are similar, with both stories culminating in rest.

Moses's origin story, the whole baby found floating alone in a basket in a river episode, fits into a larger collection of ancient Near Eastern hero origin stories that have an abandoned hero motif. Included in this collection is the story of Sargon, the ancient king of Akkad and the builder of Mesopotamia. Sargon's mother put baby Sargon in a reed basket treated with bitumen and put it in the Euphrates River. Then a person drawing water from the river found and raised him. Which sounds exactly like the Moses story.

On top of the similarity between the content of the Bible and other concurrent religious texts, modern archaeological evidence doesn't support the historicity of the Jewish people's conquest of the promised land or their departure from Egypt in the exodus. Given all the grandeur of the exodus—with its plagues, the angel of death killing the firstborns, and the splitting of the Red Sea—one would think that someone outside of Judaism would have felt the need to record the event. Yet little to no historical evidence exists outside of the Jewish account. Is it too much to ask for a biblical account to be verifiable so there is no debate over its historicity?

All of this makes me wonder whether any of the historical accounts in the Old Testament are true or whether they were just one culture's attempt to find identity and significance despite its relative weakness and inferiority.

When we get into the tenets of Christianity, I don't question whether Jesus of Nazareth existed. Enough was written about Jesus that I don't question his existence or his crucifixion. Plenty of first-century messiah figures ended up on the Romans' gruesome torture device. As troubling as the historicity of the Jewish stories and their borrowed material are to me, my question is focused singularly on Jesus's resurrection. What happened on the third day in Jesus's tomb is the linchpin of my entire faith. I'd be fine with the entire Old Testament being fan fiction if God resurrected Jesus from the dead.

The apostle Paul said that Christians are to be pitied more than all people if there is no resurrection.[1] No passage of Scripture seems more inspired than those words, because if there is no resurrection, then faith is all in vain.

The way Jesus's disciples lived (and died) after the third day convinces some people of the resurrection's truthfulness. If people were willing to die for Jesus, the argument goes, because they believed him to be resurrected, then Jesus's resurrection must be true. But if that logic holds up, then those who flew planes into the Twin Towers on 9/11 did the will of God, because they too were willing to die for what they believed.

Many people, terrorists and nonterrorists, die for beliefs that aren't true.

Some believe without question because the biblical authors say it happened, but the cynical voice in the back of my head whispers, "Sure, trust those who wrote the Bible, because *their* accounts couldn't have been altered by their bias." It's like trusting the research that says Ford makes the best trucks when the researchers all work for Ford. The biblical authors' biased testimony wouldn't convince me if I were a juror on the case for Christ.

I wonder if Jesus happened to be the one Jewish rabbi turned messianic figure who arrived at the right place and the right time. The first-century crowds were ripe for revolution when Jesus, the winsome teacher, arrived on the scene. The people's rabid desire for freedom from Roman oppression mixed with Jesus's charisma. Add a few handfuls of unintentional exaggeration plus a pinch of intentional distortions by well-meaning followers, and that conglomeration becomes the story that gets spread.

This stew of truth and distortion existed in the margins of society for a few hundred years, long enough to distance itself from the serious scrutiny of eyewitnesses. Then the Roman emperor Constantine saw a vision of the Jesus sign, the Chi Rho, in the clouds before an important battle. Constantine, superstitious man that he was, promised to dedicate his life to that sign if he won, much like a Chicago Cubs fan promising faithful church attendance for a World Series victory who then, within a year of the victory, becomes the new chair of First Baptist Church's deacon board. Constantine won the battle, and thus the most powerful person in the world became a faithful devotee of the Jesus movement. Instantly, the underground religion went mainstream, and the story became what it is today.

The perfect recipe existed for a tipping point to happen: an oppressed community, a charismatic leader, rabid devotees, a gruesome death, and a powerful convert.

I've been around long enough to see inconsequential practices and ideas converted into essential dogmas. I've seen churches believe a white cloth over a Eucharist table is a sacred ritual imbued with divine significance, even though the cloth was originally placed over the table to keep flies from getting into the bread and the wine when the churches' lack of air-conditioning required the windows to be open. In my own personal religious tradition, we developed an entire theological system for why having musical instruments in a church service is a sin despite explicit exhortation in Scripture to use musical instruments. The initial decision not to use instruments was not a biblical one but an economical one for poor Southern churches during the American Civil War. Regardless of inconvenient things like facts, groups have a propensity to turn nonessential ideas into essential dogma.

Which is why I am in a room surrounded by a thousand voices, and I'm the only one who can't sing. Because what is there to sing about?

Can we prove that God is truly a loving Father while suffering is rampant in God's created world?

Can we prove that God exists without any doubt?

Can we prove that any of it is true?

The answer for me is no. I can't prove it. I've never been able to build the wall high enough and pack it tightly enough to keep my questions on the outside. And now the water has knocked down the wall and dragged me out to sea, and I'm drowning in the unknown.

It's no wonder I can't sing—my lungs are full of doubt.

2

God Equals Good

Their first night home after their honeymoon, Paul set his alarm clock, turned off the lamp, fell onto the pillow, and said to his wife of six days, Rachel, "I've got to leave for work at six, so can you have breakfast ready by 5:45?"

"Excuse me?" Rachel said.

"5:45. I think that should be enough time for me to eat before I have to leave."

"What do you mean 'have breakfast ready'?"

"Well, my mom used to make me breakfast every morning: eggs, sausage, and homemade biscuits. So I figured you would too."

"I'm not your mom."

Paul is somehow still married, and now he's the one who cooks breakfast on our ski trips, because over the last six years, he's learned how to eat breakfast without his mother.

Who said miracles don't happen?

As the saying goes, expectations are nothing more than premeditated resentments.

If you expect your spouse to make you breakfast every morning without discussing it beforehand, you are planning for resentment. Unrealistic and unexpressed expectations can destroy a relationship with a spouse or with God.

Expectations accumulate like stains on a white couch, appearing without our knowing from where they originated. We clothe God with expectations derived from our daddy issues, Greek mythology, or the latest Morgan Freeman movie, because we all know that Morgan Freeman's voice is actually God's voice.

Those obsessed with control often develop an expectation for God to be a micromanaging deity. Those averse to judgment expect God never to step on anyone's toes. We deify what we value.

Some expectations for God come from our family of origin. Based on my own professional experience, one of the most important indicators of whether someone will have a positive relationship with God is whether they had a positive relationship with their father. Some intuitively trust God because they trusted their dad. Those who had a negative experience with their father can't have a positive relationship with God without jettisoning the ubiquitous masculine imagery for God in Scripture. While this is not fair, it's often true—just like the old saying in the world of athletics: if you want to be a good athlete, you must pick your parents well. One of the reasons the twins on my college track team were All-Americans and I was a lowly walk-on was because my dad played football until tenth grade and the twins' father played ten years for the Dallas Cowboys.

Our family of origin sets the course for much of our lives, including our relationship with our Creator. Expectations in spirituality play such a central role because we are trying to build ideas about the unknown, and it's much easier to start with what we know as the foundation.

Our church has around seventy-five refugees who are part of our community, many originally from the Democratic Republic of Congo. The names of my Congolese friends Patrick and Innocent were easy for me to learn, but Kashindi's and Ramjaane's names were a struggle because I'd never heard those words before. It's easier for me to remember "Patrick" than "Kashindi" because I'm simply associating a new face with an already known word. I'm only having to stack information, not create a new framework.

Our brains prefer the ease of accumulation instead of the struggle of creation out of nothing, so everything we see and experience shapes our understanding of God, whether we want those experiences to influence our understanding of God or not.

This is one of the lessons we've learned from physics known as observer effect—the act of observing affects any object. The standard soda taste test of Coke versus Pepsi is never done with the labels of the beverages visible to participants, because that will skew the participants' judgment. Participants will associate their previous preference with their current experience of the beverage. This is why the only type of test that has any credibility is a double-blind test, which prevents biases from corrupting the results.

Our ability to disassociate our expectations from our current experience is minimal at best, whether concerning a taste test of sodas or our description of God. Which is why all theology is to some degree autobiography.

You tell me who God is, and I can tell you your story.

We accumulate different views of gods that combine into what we call God, and the by-products of that accumulation are the expectations we bring. We then expect God to equal the composite god of our creation. Our expectations become a reservation for future disappointments with God, because God is not bound by the expectations we create for God.

"God, You Can't . . ."

Eugene Peterson wrote, "But Jesus does not always meet our expectations, does not always give what we ask for or what we think we need. When he doesn't, we feel let down, deflated, disappointed, or we surf to another channel on the TV, or we try out another church that will, hopefully, give us what we ask for."[1]

Expectations have long caused disappointment with God. God told a Jewish prophet Habakkuk that God would use the Jewish people's enemy, the Chaldeans, known by many modern scholars as the Neo-Babylonians, to destroy them.

> Look at the nations, and see!
> Be astonished! Be astounded!

> For a work is being done in your days
> > that you would not believe if you were told.
> For I am rousing the Chaldeans,
> > that fierce and impetuous nation,
> who march through the breadth of the earth
> > to seize dwellings not their own. (Hab. 1:5–6)

But then the prophet responded to God, saying,

> Your eyes are too pure to behold evil,
> > and you cannot look on wrongdoing;
> why do you look on the treacherous,
> > and are silent when the wicked swallow
> > those more righteous than they? (Hab. 1:13)

Habakkuk informed God that God couldn't allow bad things to happen to him and his people because God had to meet his definition of good.

Habakkuk ended up disappointed.

I've always liked Habakkuk, probably because the expectations we both started with for God are pretty similar. I've also expected a clearly delineated equation: God equals good, and not good equals not God.

I expected God to show up and turn every bad situation good and every good situation even better.

Deus ex Machina

When ancient playwrights faced an unsalvageable conflict, some gave in to the cheap temptation to use the divine as a panacea for poorly constructed plots. The divine would descend into the bottlenecked story to resolve the problem. Because the divine would be lowered on an actual machine, this move was described using the Latin phrase *deus ex machina*.[2]

When the story was jammed, it was time to call in the divine to do the unnatural. When they couldn't figure out how to resolve a conflict, they brought in God.

But the tactic wasn't used only by ancient playwrights; modern screenwriters are guilty of this too. In 1978, Patrick Duffy played a main character named Bobby Ewing on the extremely popular soap opera *Dallas*, but Duffy wanted off the show. So the writers ended that year's season, the show's seventh, with Bobby Ewing's death. Fans of the show were furious because they loved Bobby Ewing and didn't want him gone. The producers listened to the fans and got Duffy back on board for season eight, but Duffy's character, Bobby Ewing, had already died.

How do you bring back a character who's dead—well, besides resurrection, since the Bible already told that story? In typical *deus ex machina* fashion, *Dallas* started season eight with Bobby walking out of the bathroom to tell his startled and just awoken wife that his death and all that had occurred in season seven had just been a dream that she had been given from above. The divine had swooped in to give the viewers the Pollyanna resolution they wanted.

When the divine is lowered down into our world, everything becomes good.

God's appearance means good, and God's absence means bad.

"God showed up." In my younger days, I'd use this phrase when referencing the unforeseeable turn of a bad situation into a good situation, which basically turned God into a delivery service for good circumstances.

But to be fair, sometimes that's how life works.

The story of the Jewish hero Joseph perpetuates this view of God showing up and taking what was intended for bad and making it good. Joseph's brothers disliked him, probably because of their father's blatant favoritism and Joseph's lack of humility. So the brothers sold him off to be a slave, which, in comparison, makes that time when I was six and hit my brother with a two-by-four, causing him to need five stitches, seem not so bad. Joseph became an Egyptian slave because of his brothers, but his life continued to get worse. Because of Joseph's unwillingness to be a boy toy for his boss's wife, who claimed Joseph assaulted her, Joseph was sent to prison. While in prison, Joseph befriended one of the king's right-hand men, and because of Joseph's ability to interpret dreams, his new friend called upon Joseph to help the king. Joseph rightly predicted a famine, which elevated Joseph from a prisoner to the second most powerful man in Egypt. Joseph saved the Egyptians and his own Jewish people.

God was the *deus ex machina* for Joseph.

And God was the *deus ex machina* for the family of my friend Mitch, who sent me this text message.

Pray for my mom. She's been shot with an
arrow in her neck.

I strongly believe that God intended most communication to occur through text messages, not phone calls. If God wanted us to talk instead of text, then why did God give us one mouth but ten fingers? That's just math.

But a message about someone being shot with an arrow in the neck is the rare exception when a phone call is warranted.

Mitch's mom had stepped outside her Amarillo, Texas, home onto her porch, where she stood underneath her roof, in between two hanging plants, and behind waist-high bushes. While she was standing there, an arrow flew under the roof, in between the hanging plants, and over the bushes, hitting her in the neck.

She stumbled inside her house, arrow still in her neck, to her husband, who had to be just a bit confused as to why his wife looked like an actor from *Braveheart*.

At the hospital, the doctors discovered that the arrow was a practice arrow, which meant it didn't have the blades of a hunting arrow. She was lucky (or at least as lucky as one can be when they have an arrow in their neck) that it wasn't a hunting arrow, which would have caused substantially more damage. But her luck didn't stop there. If the arrow had landed millimeters away, it would have hit her jugular vein, which would have caused her to bleed out before she ever arrived at the hospital. The doctors successfully removed the practice arrow. But the story doesn't end there.

A little investigation proved that the fateful arrow had been purchased at the only store in that town selling arrows, which just happened to be owned by my friend's brother, aka the victim's other son. This small fact instantly made my friend the favorite son in the family, since he hadn't sold the arrow that had hit his mom in the neck. Until the CAT scan came back.

The CAT scan, which was run to ensure that no internal damage had occurred during the surgery, revealed that she had a previously undetected brain tumor that was about to cause a life-ending stroke. The doctor caught it in time and successfully performed brain surgery.

But the story doesn't end there.

Three years later she returned for her yearly brain scan, and the doctor detected another abnormality. This time a brain vessel was about to burst, which would have caused a brain aneurysm. They performed a second successful brain surgery, and for the second time, her life was saved because of the arrow.

Who would have thought that the thing that would save my friend's mom's life from a brain tumor and a brain aneurysm would be an arrow, from her son's store, that flew under the roof, through the hanging plants, and over bushes to impale her in the neck?

God took what was meant for bad and made it good.

But many times the good never comes and the bad situation isn't reframed. When we have an expectation for a *deus ex machina* God, God doesn't equal good. God is just the vehicle to get what we determined to be good. And when God is just the vehicle that carries the good circumstances, and those good circumstances don't arrive, what does that say about God?

We end up sounding like the Jewish prophet Habakkuk: "But, God, you are too pure to let this happen."

Rocky Runs

Unmet expectations don't *have* to turn into resentment. We can just pretend they don't exist. We can bury them under the business of life and hope they never reemerge.

I was speaking with a pastor friend about the authorship of the first five books of the Old Testament—you know, the typical nerdy discussions pastors have. Those books, often called the Pentateuch or the Books of Moses, claim Moses as their author, though there are some issues with Moses being the author in the way that a twenty-first-century person would understand authorship.

The Pentateuch refers to cities that weren't founded and people groups that arrived after Moses's lifetime. Deuteronomy 34 describes Moses's death, which would have been difficult for him to write about if he were in fact dead.

But most troubling, at least to me, is Moses writing about himself in the fourth book of the Pentateuch: "Now the man Moses was very humble, more so than anyone else on the face of the earth" (Num. 12:3).

Moses wrote that he was the humblest man on earth? That just doesn't seem right.

I mentioned a prominent non-Moses authorship option to my friend. He said, "I don't like that theory because it makes less of God." He didn't doubt the truthfulness of the theory; he didn't accept it because it disrupted his expectations for God.

He picked a pretty common option in the face of broken expectations: ignore. Act like the inconsistencies don't exist because reality reduces our image of who God is supposed to be. Ignoring does work for a while. And for some, it can work forever.

When a tiny rock gets in your shoe while you're out for a run, if it wiggles down into just the right spot, it can go unnoticed for the entirety of the run. But more often than not, the rock gets lodged somewhere painful, like directly under your heel. Every time your foot strikes the ground, the rock digs into your foot, making the next step impossible. The only way to continue is to deal with the issue.

Not dealing with the difficulties or the disappointments we have with God means there will always be, at the relationship's core, something between us and God. We can do all the right things and read all the right verses and sing all the right songs, but they won't dissolve the tension in the relationship.

When broken expectations fracture the unity in our relationship with God, the only way back to unity with God is through facing those disappointments. It's here that faith either grows or dies.

We must choose wisely before entering into the disappointments, though most us don't have a choice.

Experience

Charles Darwin, in his pivotal work, *The Origin of Species*, laid out the mechanism for evolution that many use as the proverbial nail in the coffin of Christianity. If we assume that evolution happened, then God didn't create the world in six days, and thus the entire Bible falls apart. The argument goes that if the first chapter of Genesis isn't a literal historical and scientific account, then it's useless, along with the other 1,188 chapters in the Bible. The fact that God could orchestrate evolution and that the first chapter of Genesis could be a theological affirmation rather than a historical account isn't even an option in this view. The common story goes that Darwin's science destroyed his faith and the faith of everyone else who encounters Darwin's work while also starting a bumper-sticker war between the Jesus fish and the Darwin amphibian.

But some believe Charles Darwin's faith didn't collapse because of any of his discoveries in a laboratory but because of what happened in a hospital. According to this take, Darwin's faith devolved when his ten-year-old daughter, Anne Elizabeth, got sick and ultimately passed away from what some now believe to have been tuberculosis. Darwin was so understandably shaken that he couldn't even attend Anne's funeral. Only after her death did Darwin become vocal about his religious doubts.

Suffering changes us in a way that nothing else can.

I would like to think that humans are calculating beings who make rational decisions, as Aristotle said we do, but the human experience is far more complex than that. Intellectual issues are significant, but they cannot be divorced from experience. Sometimes suffering amplifies preexisting doubts; other times suffering creates doubts. If suffering teaches us anything, it's that we aren't simply what we think—we are also what we experience.

For some, a dramatic wave of suffering knocks down their spiritual sandcastle. For me, the slow, steady seepage washed away my naive and idealistic expectations.

I first noticed the leak in my faith in seminary, when my expectations for what I wanted the Bible to be didn't match what it really was. I wanted the Bible to be a direct message from God to us without the messy trappings of people. I wanted inspiration to transcend humanity by way of a divine light from heaven shooting down into the biblical authors, in a reverse demon-possession-type move. The divine light controlling the authors' hands as they wrote the Bible with an unquestionable legitimacy. I wanted a divide between the divine and the human, but that's not what I got.

When couples fall in love, they usually fall in love with the idea of love rather than with the actual person. Love's intoxicants blur our ability to see the object of our affection clearly, and so we love the fantasy we've created about that person. Fantasy doesn't allow for honest humanity, but eventually we sober up and get to know the human in front of us. We find out they are a mixture of dust and divine.

Sinner and saint.

Beauty and brokenness.

And it's then that we must decide if we will choose real love or if we will walk away because we are more committed to the ideal than the real.

Suffering is often when we sober up to who God actually is and not just what we expect God to be. And then we must decide to stay or let our faith be washed away.

Sliding to Cynicism

Church historian and biblical scholar N. T. Wright told me in a podcast that the Lisbon earthquake of 1755 destroyed the idea that anyone could plainly see the Christian God simply by looking around.[3] To which I nodded and said, "Hmm . . . yeah," while I quietly googled "Lisbon+Earthquake+1755."

> On All Saints Day, three tremors over the course of 10 minutes suddenly struck Lisbon. The worst of the quakes is thought to

have had a magnitude of 8.0, though this is just an estimate as no recording equipment existed at the time. The shaking was felt as far away as Morocco.

The devastating effects of the earthquake were felt throughout the city. Close to the coast, a 20-foot tsunami rushed ashore and killed thousands. Many people were observing All Saints Day in churches at the time and died when the buildings collapsed. Fires broke out all over the city and winds spread the flames quickly. The royal palace was destroyed, as were thousands of homes. Much of the country's cultural history, preserved in books, art and architecture, was wiped away in an instant. Many of the city's residents, including hundreds of escaped prisoners, fled Lisbon immediately. The death toll has been estimated at between 10,000 and 50,000.[4]

After that schooling by Wikipedia, once again Rev. Wright and I were in full agreement.

The suffering caused by the tragic earthquake sobered many Christians as to who God is and who God isn't. The *deus ex machina* God disappeared, and many turned to deism, which is the idea that God is the watchmaker who created us, set the world in motion, and then left us on our own.

The faith of many people becomes otherworldly because of suffering, whether that be the "Jesus is only trying to get you into heaven" otherworldliness or the "this world is too messy for an active God" deism otherworldliness.

This is what my faith slid into: deism. Deism with a heavy dose of cynicism, to be precise.

I was like the trite characters in romantic comedies who act as if they don't need or want to be loved but eventually let their guard down to reveal wounds from the past that caused them to keep their distance. I was basically the female lead in every Matthew McConaughey movie from the early 2000s.

My heart would become a seething ball of anger when someone said that God had blessed them with a promotion or that God had protected them from a natural disaster, because I was thinking of the person "blessed" with getting fired who made the promotion available or the person whose home the tornado had destroyed.

I was a nice enough pastor, never (knowingly) attempting to correct a parishioner's willingness to attribute good fortune to God's hand. But that courtesy wasn't extended to my own family. My dad is a cancer survivor who has spent his life helping people with chronic pain professionally and being married to my mom, who for most of my lifetime has had a chronic illness. It's not as if he's lived a charmed life untouched by suffering. Nevertheless, I didn't want to let his wisdom get in the way of my need to correct his flawed attribution of blessing to God.

I knew I had a problem when my dad began putting caveats in before he attributed anything to God.

"Now, Luke, I don't understand how God works, and so I can't say for sure this is true, but I think this was a real blessing. . . ."

When your father has to include a preamble to qualify his gratitude for a good outcome at a cancer checkup, you've got an issue.

My wife is a neonatal intensive care unit nurse, and I'm fairly certain that she does more important work than I do, as conversations like the following indicate:

"Lindsay, how was work today?"

"Good. I had a two-pound baby addicted to cocaine who kept trying to die on me. We brought him back to life three times."

"That's cool. Do you want to guess what cool thing I did today?"

"I don't know, Luke. Just tell me."

"I got retweeted by N. T. Wright. So, sweetheart, I guess both of us had pretty big days."

I've never been one to let something as silly as humility get in the way of my ability to express how I had God figured out more than anyone, including my wife. She might want to say that God saved a premature, drug-addicted baby, but I'd be quick to let her know that if God didn't also save every other baby, then he wasn't being fair.

The thing about cynicism is that cynicism is never satisfied.

Cynicism never reaches a threshold where it's content with how much it has altered our perspective on the world. Cynicism doesn't stop when it has corrupted enough of our essential relationships. It continues unchained by a concern for our well-being. Cynicism incessantly interrupts our most basic and foundational beliefs with, "Can you really trust that?" Even while I was preaching, cynicism would slip a thought into my head: "Are you really sure about what you just said?" Cynicism is never satisfied. It continues to scrape away anything living in the soul until there are no more signs of life.

At my lowest point, I had no expectations for God because I didn't want to be disappointed again. My expectations for God's involvement in the world and in my life had become almost nonexistent, because you can't be disappointed if you don't expect anything.

Miroslav Volf said that the great temptation isn't worshiping false gods but to live by bread alone, to live as though the material world is all that exists.[5] And that's what my belief had devolved into: a distant God who didn't show up anymore, leaving the material world and me as all that existed. As cynicism gnawed away at my soul, I was defenseless, especially because, a few years prior, I had lost my most life-giving practice.

Stop Reading the Bible

"Luke, you know you don't have to read your Bible every day to be a Christian."

A grace-filled, true statement has never been more destructive to me.

My friend Chris, who said those words, will probably not remember those words being spoken. But I can't forget them, because I was not the same after hearing them.

During my sophomore year in college, I applied for a summer youth ministry internship at a great church in Atlanta. I didn't have any interest in youth ministry as a career. My high rate of grumpiness when I didn't get enough sleep created a very real possibility that I could go postal on a middle-school boy who thought it was cool to prank the youth ministry intern. But I assumed that I could survive ten weeks of youth ministry while maintaining my nonviolent convictions, so I went ahead and applied for one of the two male youth ministry positions.

The church offered the positions to me and a freshman at my college named Chris, whom I didn't know. This was pre-Facebook, so I couldn't just look him up online. And cell phones weren't around, so I couldn't text him either. It was a very dark time when people actually had to interact with each other in person using actual words. So we set up a time to meet in person, like two cavemen.

Turns out we were a bit different.

The private Christian school we attended didn't have fraternities, but it had their equivalent (with significantly fewer keg parties), which we called social clubs. My club consisted mainly of the preppy jock types who wore a lot of Abercrombie & Fitch clothing, which was a somewhat fair description of me in college. I had walked on to the university's track team, though I was nowhere near good enough to be on a team that had four athletes run in the Olympics in Atlanta the year before.

Chris, on the other hand, was not the preppy jock type. Instead, Chris was into wearing white T-shirts that he wrote on with markers, eating vegan food, and listening to hardcore music—a style of music that I wasn't too familiar with but seemed to be simply a lot of yelling, mostly about how terrible preppy jock types who wore Abercrombie clothing were. And thus the reason I had never met Chris.

Nevertheless, we somehow became friends—actually good friends. We learned to find a middle ground. I started listening to his music, and he started showering.

After the ten-week internship ended, we returned to school in Texas, and our bromance bloomed. After my junior year of college began, I started preaching at a small country church forty-five minutes outside of town. Within a year, Chris started going out to this church with me. He would teach the Sunday school class, and I would preach. On the drive home, we would criticize each other's performance in the name of love and sophomoric wisdom.

Chris is smart, like after he finished his master's degree he got into Harvard smart. The sheer abundance of dumb stuff that I said as a nineteen-year-old preacher and his intelligence gave him plenty to criticize.

In one conversation, Chris made an offhand comment about how we often reduce Christianity down to just reading our Bible every day. Following Jesus is supposed to have an all-encompassing impact on someone's life, not just be a fifteen-minute task in the morning. Christianity isn't just about reading the Bible, which is a good thing for the majority of Christians throughout history who didn't have access to a Bible before the invention of the printing press five hundred years ago. So of course Christianity isn't just about reading the Bible.

But I lost the entire forest for one little tree. "You know you don't have to read your Bible every day to be a Christian."

That day I stopped my daily Bible reading. We are what we do repeatedly, and what was lost wasn't a legalistic religious conviction; it was a building block for my identity.

Andrew Newberg, a neuroscientist at Thomas Jefferson University Hospital and a professor, in the book *How God Changes Your Brain*, said:

> Our research team at the University of Pennsylvania has consistently demonstrated that God is part of our consciousness and that the more you think about God, the more you will alter the neural circuitry in specific parts of your brain. That is why I say, with the utmost confidence, that God can change

your brain. And it doesn't matter if you're a Christian or a Jew, a Muslim or a Hindu, or an agnostic or an atheist.[6]

The brain is altered by the idea of God through a process called neuroplasticity, which Newberg described as the human brain's ability to structurally rearrange itself in response to a wide variety of positive and negative events. Newberg went on to say:

> So what does neuroplasticity have to do with God? Everything, for if you contemplate something as complex or mysterious as God, you're going to have incredible bursts of neural activity firing in different parts of your brain. New dendrites will rapidly grow and old associations will disconnect as new imaginative perspectives emerge. In essence, when you think about the really big questions in life—be they religious, scientific, or psychological—your brain is going to grow.[7]

So if I understand neuroplasticity correctly, which my B in Biology 101 freshman year would confirm, our brains change and create new connections when we meditate on God, as I was doing when I was reading my Bible. But when we stop using the "God part" of our brains, they revert back to pre-God brains.

Neuroplasticity explains the biology behind what I had already come to know. When I stopped practicing the discipline that changed my brain, my faith slipped away and the crack in the wall grew.

The Emptiness

The practice of Bible reading for me was less about the acquisition of intellectual concepts and more about character formation. It shaped my person more than my mind. What I lost wasn't ideas about God but my connection to God. It was as if that part of my brain was slowly being disconnected, and a void in my soul developed.

Many believe the tradition of saying "God bless you" when someone sneezes comes from a rather odd application of Matthew 12:43–45:

> When the unclean spirit has gone out of a person, it wanders through waterless regions looking for a resting place, but it finds none. Then it says, "I will return to my house from which I came." When it comes, it finds it empty, swept, and put in order. Then it goes and brings along seven other spirits more evil than itself, and they enter and live there; and the last state of that person is worse than the first. So will it be also with this evil generation.

When someone sneezed, the ancient belief was that an evil spirit would leave the sneezer's soul, but if the magical phrase wasn't uttered, the void would be occupied by seven more evil spirits.[8] I say "Bless you" out of courtesy, not because I believe spirits are waiting for the opportune moment, like kids playing double Dutch, timing the jump rope's rotation before they jump in. But the principle remains true.

Emptiness makes the heart grow fonder for anything that fills the void. For me, the emptiness made room for cynicism to grow in my heart. And it bloomed.

3

Binary to Beauty

Once upon a time there was a guy named Bobby who lived on the beach—not living on the beach as in owning a Malibu beachfront house but more like Tom Hanks in the movie *Castaway*.

No one ever told Bobby about the danger of the water, but then again, no lessons were required on undertows or riptides or sharks. He developed a fear of the water on his own. The sight of the wall of water slamming down, the sound of the crashing waves, and thoughts about what lurked beneath the water instilled enough trepidation within Bobby that he didn't go anywhere near the water. But despite his fear, Bobby couldn't take his eyes off the water.

He set out to barricade himself from the water using the only thing he had—sand. He stacked the sand as deep and as high as he could, making the sturdiest sandcastle possible. Smoothing out every rough edge and perfecting every surface made him feel safe, but he didn't like not being able to see the water. When his curiosity would get the best of him, he would burrow out a peephole, steal a glance at the water, then refill the hole.

Despite his best efforts, the water wouldn't stay outside the wall. Water would drip on his head while he slept, and he would step in a puddle when he awoke. Every day he would leave the security of the wall to gather more sand to repair the wall to keep the water at bay.

Early one morning during his gathering sand routine, Bobby noticed all the seagulls flying away and the tide recessing far from the shore. A quiet covered the beach, and for a moment, he felt relaxed by the peacefulness of a still dawn.

His glance out to the ocean washed away all serenity. A lone, rogue wave towered over the ocean, streaking toward the shore.

He dropped the sand and sprinted to get to the castle. Adrenaline coursed through his veins, sending his muscles into a panic-stricken flight to get to safety.

As he jumped behind the barricade and put his back against the sandy wall, a deep breath filling his lungs, he smirked as he thought, *Yet again, I've mastered the water.*

Then his perfectly smooth wall flattened him as the rogue wave slammed against the sandcastle, which didn't have a chance. Bobby was knocked forward in the wash of sand and saltwater, spinning and slamming him into the beach.

Then the wave began to recede back into the ocean, and the water pulled him out to sea like a scaly claw pulling you out of your tent at night. He grasped for anything to hold on to, but the sand was no friend in this battle. He went farther and farther into the ocean and farther and farther away from what he knew. He gasped for a breath of air, but his lungs filled with saltwater.

Upside down in the full spin cycle of the dark abyss, he thought, *This was bound to happen. I never stood a chance.*

He accepted this to be his end. The shore was no longer visible, and he couldn't keep fighting the current. So he stopped. No more thrashing. No more reaching. No more gasping. He closed his eyes and let go.

Of course I couldn't keep the water away forever. This was bound to happen.

As his inner dialogue whimpered over and over again, Bobby realized something. He was still alive. He opened his eyes to see that the water had lifted him to the surface. He was nowhere near the shore, but he was nowhere near dead either.

The water wasn't drowning him.

This wasn't killing water.

It was living water.

Into the Water

Jesus said that if you want to save your life, you must lose it.[1]

Spirituality is about letting go, but spirituality cannot start with letting go, because we can't give away what we don't possess. Spirituality begins with constructing what will eventually be cast aside, like training wheels on a child's bicycle. What we start with on our spiritual journey has a valuable purpose, but it cannot stay forever.

We begin life with the chaotic waters crashing near our feet. The God we've fashioned into the mold of our expectations becomes the sandcastle keeping away the unpleasant unknown. We develop an appreciation for the sandcastle's protection, but it can become a hindrance for our next step in maturity. The invitation into the mystery persists despite our best attempts to keep God in our well-defined boxes, because we can't keep the all-present God out.

When I was a college senior contemplating seminary, a slightly older preacher, who didn't go to seminary, warned me not to go to seminary unless I was "called" to go to seminary because he had seen a lot of guys lose their love for the Lord in seminary. He was basically saying, "Your understanding of God could be rattled in seminary, so stay on the shore."

His warning rightly acknowledged a deconstruction process that often happens in seminary (just as it happens for non-seminarians other places in life), but he didn't leave room for the reconstruction that could also happen.

The "stay on the shore" impulse confuses curiosity about God with unfaithfulness to God, because on the shore, the main goal is to stay dry.

Drowning in Dominoes

Once in the water, we try to get back to where we were on the land. We repeat the same practices that worked before, but like trying to put toothpaste back into the tube, they just don't work. It's here that we realize we can't go back, so we must find a way to sink or swim in this newfound reality.

Far too many can't swim because they have domino faith.

When I was a kid, our family used to play dominoes, though my interest in dominoes was centered on what I got to do with the dominoes after the game concluded. Once the scores were tallied and the victor proclaimed, the table emptied and I would get to be alone with the dominoes to have some real fun.

I would develop elaborate lines with those ivory beauties, stacking them, spiraling them, and staircasing them all over the table, all the while evading the destructive force of my older brother, who finds no greater joy in life than seeing people suffer, specifically his younger sibling. He would clandestinely come around the corner to destroy my work with one finger. He wouldn't have to push every domino down individually for all the dominoes to fall. All he would need to do was bump one domino, then one by one all would come crashing down.

One domino's downfall equaled the destruction of all the dominoes, which for too many people describes the structure that sustains their view of the divine. All tenets are equally important, and without one, they all come crashing down. This view of beliefs leads to the ever popular slippery slope argument in religious communities. If belief A isn't true, then belief B isn't true, then belief C and all beliefs all the way to Z aren't true. Domino faith turns religion into a zero-sum game, and it turns many of us into atheists when we end up in the water.

Far too many people leave the faith because if they can't keep all their beliefs, then they can't keep any of them. Unlike the apostle Paul, who could see that some beliefs and expectations were of first importance, they see them all equally.

Floating

When we enter the water, we initially try to get back to shore, to the way things used to be. If we are wise, we stop fighting the water and accept it as that which keeps us afloat. We acknowledge that the water isn't destroying water; it's living water.

This is not an anti-intellectualism that runs away from serious theological discussion or thoughtful inquiry into the divine. It's an acknowledgment of the human inability to know everything. It means, as the apostle Paul said, that what we see now is a dim reflection, but one day we will see face-to-face. What we know now is partial but one day will be full.[2]

Looking through dim light and knowing with only partial knowledge create a humble realization that we aren't an all-knowing expert but a fellow swimmer in the mystery. So we learn to love those swimming in the mystery with us.

Just Another Monday

It would be great if there was one life-changing moment that instilled faith, but life doesn't work that way for most of us. There might be a moment when we realize a change has happened, but that change usually takes place over weeks, months, or years, not in a singular moment.

It's like swimming.

I first started swimming consistently when I was in my midtwenties, because it seemed to be the type of activity that wouldn't destroy my joints. On the first Monday in the lap pool, I struggled to swim one lap with my glorified dog paddle.

But I kept showing up, Monday after Monday.

When I was in my early thirties, some friends asked me to do the 1.2-mile open-water swim leg in a triathlon relay. I never could have done that a decade before, but I was able to do it without any substantial change to what I was doing every Monday at the pool.

I don't know exactly when I stopped being a drowning hazard. The change just happened during one of those boring Mondays in the pool. It wasn't a spectacular moment, just another Monday.

The same is true for spiritual maturity. We would like a giant leap from expectation to acceptance, but that's not the way of growth. Growth happens during normal, boring Mondays.

Hands on the Wheel

I don't watch NASCAR, but my grandma does. So this next story goes out to you, Grandma. Enjoy.

In the 146th lap of the 2014 Daytona 500, a thirteen-car accident occurred, ending the race for a handful of drivers, including one driver even non-NASCAR fans know, Danica Patrick. Up until then, Patrick appeared to be on her way to a respectable top-twenty finish, but the collision sent her car toward the wall. Naturally, she fought to keep her car away from the wall but with no success.

A split second before the collision with the wall, she did the strangest thing: she released her hands from the steering wheel.

When Patrick's car crashed into the wall, the steering wheel violently twisted with such great torque that it would have snapped almost any athlete's wrists if their hands had been wrapped around the wheel. Patrick saved her wrists by letting go of the wheel.

Sometimes the only thing that can save us is letting go.

To save her wrists, Patrick had to let go.

To save our faith, some of us must do the same thing with our expectations.

Like Jesus said, if we want to save our life, we must lose it. Salvation or control—if we want one, then we can't have the other. We can keep gripping the steering wheel of how we think life, God, and the universe should function, or we can have salvation. We can't have both.

It's a choice: expectations or faith.

The Only Thing That Can Save Us

My first job out of school took me to the beautiful white sandy beaches of Florida's Gulf Coast, where I struck up a brief relationship with kitesurfing. It never really got serious. It was really just a bad first date, followed by a few weeks of both of us knowing the relationship wasn't going anywhere.

If you've never seen kitesurfing, imagine someone on an oversized floating skateboard in the water being pulled by a half parachute. It's a bit more complicated than that, but that's the basic idea: big kite, small board, some wires, and, oh yeah, water and wind.

A kitesurfer is connected to the kite by three cords that attach to the belt they wear. Connected to those cords is a two-foot-long bar. When you are being pulled across the water, the bar is the only thing you can hold on to, so you're often tricked into thinking the bar is there to help keep you standing, but it's not.

Whenever I felt like I was going too fast and about to fall, I would do the natural thing: pull on the bar extremely hard so I wouldn't fall into the water and get eaten by a shark. Herein lies the problem: pulling back on the bar doesn't fix the problem; it amplifies the problem.

The bar isn't a handle. It's a throttle.

When you are losing control and you pull back on the bar, the action pulls the edges of the kite down, causing them to catch more wind, thus making you go faster.

Every time I was out of control and going too fast, I would instinctively pull on the bar, and then I would go faster, so I would hit the water harder, creating a bigger splash, so more sharks would know I was ready to be eaten.

When things are spiraling out of control, the most unnatural thing to do is to let go, but that act of relinquishing control might be the only thing that can save us.

I Kissed Controlling Good-bye

My friend Tiffany was perusing through an online dating site when she found one gentleman who had some pretty specific expectations for possible dates. If entitlement could earn someone a gold medal, he would be the Michael Phelps of online dating. Tiffany was nice enough to send a screen shot of his description to Lindsay and me, and I am nice enough to give you a brief recapitulation of his expectations.

This gentleman demanded that any lady lucky enough to be his girlfriend needed a credit score over 800, a four-bedroom home, a blood pressure of 120 over 80, no debt, and a love of cooking, cleaning, and exercise. He did graciously say that if this lucky lady met all the categories but didn't like to work out, he would settle for someone who didn't work out as long as she looked as though she liked to work out.

What a gem.

This guy was in his forties, which is not a death sentence regarding love by any means. But when you are that adamant about a person checking all your preconceived boxes, you just might be facing a death sentence; once you get beyond the basics of similar religion, family expectations, and desired location of home and into blood pressure and body fat percentages, you are displaying the selfish tendencies that destroy relationships. When things start getting away from us, we pull on the handle for more control and end up crashing even harder.

That happens in romantic relationships and in relationships with the divine.

If you want to know what your expectations are, fill in the following equation: If I _____, then God will _____.

For many, the equation looks like this:

If I go to church, then God will keep my family healthy.

If I study the Bible enough, then I will have no doubts about God.

If I pray, then my spouse will always stay.

If I do the right things, then the right things will happen to me.

God did not sign a contract spelling out how God is supposed to act during adversity. The Bible is under no legal obligation to operate in my preferred way. God did not make a pact to meet our needs of clarity and to abolish ambiguity. But that doesn't stop us from holding on to the expectations we've created or accumulated for God.

To save our life, we must lose it.

To save our faith, we must lose control.

Or as Barbara Brown Taylor says, we don't ever lose control; we only lose the illusion we ever had control.[3]

So maybe the better way to say this would be, "To save our faith, we must lose the illusion of our control." This doesn't mean we let go of God; it means we let go of our ownership of what God is.

McDonald's Grief

Maybe I was able to let go because the cynicism had dried up my soul and I had no song to sing.

Maybe it was because I couldn't get past the basic Dr. Phil question "How is this working out for you?" with a passable answer.

Maybe it was because I knew it had come down to either losing my expectations or losing my faith.

Whatever causes us to get to the point of letting go, doing so still won't be easy. Letting go isn't easy because it means letting go of who we expected God to be and how we expected our lives to go. In some ways, it's like a death that requires us to mourn the loss of who we thought God was supposed to be. If we don't grieve, we can't move past the loss. Grieving allows us to close a chapter so we can eventually open a new chapter.

My friend Betty worked with teenagers who were losing their eyesight, a bitter pill for anyone to swallow but especially a kid. Betty, who is also blind, told me that in the program, they referred to the teenagers who were not properly grieving their loss as having McDonald's grief, because they were just driving through it.

McDonald's grief is like taking only the first pill of a prescription of antibiotics; taking one pill actually makes the situation worse than if we hadn't taken any pills. Not dealing with the grief allows the grief to mutate into something even stronger. Unhealthy and incomplete mourning makes room for cynicism to take up permanent residency in the soul. The negativity we thought we dealt with was never flushed out.

I needed to grieve all that God was never going to be for me. I had to make peace with a few realities:

God is not the *deus ex machina* deity I wanted God to be.

God's sacred text is not as black and white as I assumed it to be.

God's church is not unscathed by the messiness of humanity.

God will not give me a sign that will remove all my doubts.

God will not give me the simplistic binary of God-equals-good and not-God-equals-not-good that I desired.

But upon letting go of what I expected God to be, I was able to accept what God is.

The choice will always be between keeping our old expectations or finding new ways of acceptance. We can't have both expectations and acceptance.

Once I found acceptance, I became aware of a world of goodness on the other side of cynicism.

Missing the Beauty

Some of my favorite parts of living in Florida were the scenic views and the beautiful white sandy beaches of the Gulf Coast. The home of our friends Jerry and June sits on a beautiful waterfront piece of property. Their backyard looks like a postcard complete with palm trees, a touch of white sand, and a scenic wooden boat dock. Almost every evening the sun drops down directly behind their back window, turning the bay into a heavenly palette of oranges, reds, and blues. The view out their bay window is a sight most people experience only on vacation or on a poster with a quote like "The first step to achieving is dreaming."

Nearly every evening Jerry and June gather for dinner around the kitchen table. The same table where their children ate, now their grandchildren eat.

One evening their son, Rex, noticed something troubling about their evening ritual. Jerry and June sat at the end of the table watching the news on a twenty-inch television with their backs facing the window that revealed the sunset falling over the water.

Every evening this couple watched a twenty-inch screen instead of a picturesque sunset. The beauty of creation was always right there around them; they just didn't have the right posture to be aware of it.

Is this not the problem with many marriages?

Day in and day out, we are in the presence of our spouse's beauty. But the days, weeks, months, years, and decades we've shared together erode our awareness of their beauty. We get used to how they sacrifice for the family. The hours they invest in making a child's birthday party a spectacle become expected. The way they read stories to the kids with the enthusiasm of an actor audition-ing for a Scorsese movie even when they are exhausted from a long day of work becomes the norm. The way they continually put the family's interests before their own is just par for the course.

We become acclimated and turn our backs to the beauty that's around us because we expect it to always be there.

I have never read a book, heard a sermon, or listened to a lecture that articulated the love of God better than the way in which my wife loves our daughters. But it is still easy for me to get used to the divinity in her and miss the beauty.

When we begin to ruthlessly eliminate our expectations, our eyes open to the beauty in everything around us. But as long as our hands are clenched around our expectations, we will not be open to receive God for who God is because we will be constantly comparing God to our definition of what a good God should be.

God Showed Up

In my expectations, God equaled good times. So it was only in the good times that God showed up.

The phrase "God showed up" gets casually passed around in Christian circles. People usually use it to describe how things miraculously turned out for the better. Like when a rogue arrow flies into your neck, not killing you but revealing a small but previously undetected brain tumor and thus saves your life.

You know, that kind of stuff.

"God showed up" in its simplicity is a beautiful way to express gratitude and acknowledge a source of goodness that's larger than ourselves, and I believe that's what the majority of people mean by that phrase. But when one begins to question the when, where, and how of God showing up, the phrase becomes deeply problematic.

If God showed up when things were good, what about when things weren't good?

If God shows up at certain times, does that mean that God isn't present at other times?

I heard a church leader make a statement about how we should plan worship services not to attract other people but to attract God. Which brings up questions about when God is present.

Is God like the woman on ABC's *The Bachelorette*, needing to be wined and dined so that he will join us for a hometown date, i.e., a worship service?

Is God like Beetlejuice, who shows up only if his name is said three times?

Is God the cool uncle who shows up only a couple times a year?

If God is present only in good times, then the issue moves beyond God's questionable attendance habits to the character of God.

Is God just a fair-weather friend? When we've got free food or an extra ticket to the big game, somehow they appear. But when it's time for us to move or when our car breaks down, they somehow are nowhere to be found.

Is that God?

God Is Everywhere

The Jewish texts disagree with this notion of God's capricious presence.

> Where can I go from your spirit?
>   Or where can I flee from your presence?
> If I ascend to heaven, you are there;
>   if I make my bed in Sheol, you are there.
> If I take the wings of the morning
>   and settle at the farthest limits of the sea,
> even there your hand shall lead me,
>   and your right hand shall hold me fast.
> If I say, "Surely the darkness shall cover me,
>   and the light around me become night,"
> even the darkness is not dark to you;
>   the night is as bright as the day,
>   for darkness is as light to you. (Ps. 139:7–12)

Paul echoed the same sentiment in one of his sermons:

From one ancestor he made all nations to inhabit the whole earth, and he allotted the times of their existence and the boundaries of the places where they would live, so that they would search for God and perhaps grope for him and find him—though indeed he is not far from each one of us. For "In him we live and move and have our being"; as even some of your own poets have said, "For we too are his offspring." (Acts 17:26–28)

The problem isn't that God chooses not to show up. From the Jewish texts to the story of Jesus, God is revealed as the one who is present in the darkest chapters. God isn't the cool uncle who shows up only a couple times a year. God is the faithful parent who is with us in every moment of life. God is the faithful spouse in our illness to whom the words "Visiting Hours" do not apply. God is the ever-present divine love.

The real problem is that God has shown up, but we've missed him.

Like the couple with the scenic view who've grown accustomed to the beauty around them, we sit unaware of the presence of God that's all around.

C. S. Lewis said, "We may ignore, but we can nowhere evade, the presence of God. The world is crowded with him. He walks everywhere incognito. And the incognito is not always hard to penetrate. The real labor is to remember, to attend. In fact to come awake. Still more, to remain awake."[4]

Alcoholics Anonymous teaches that one's serenity is inversely proportional to one's expectations. Our serenity is like our awareness. Our awareness of God is inversely proportional to our expectations of God. The lower our fabricated expectations for God, the more we are able to see how God is always present.

I stared at the proverbial small screen instead of the beautiful sunset behind me because God didn't meet my expectations.

As Rumi, a thirteenth-century mystic, once said, we go searching throughout our house for a diamond necklace that's been around our neck the entire time. I was too busy being upset that God wasn't where God was supposed to be or acting as God was supposed to act that I missed the beauty of how God was acting all around me.

When the first Russian cosmonaut entered space in 1961, he declared, "I don't see God up here." Seven years later, when the Americans landed on the moon, they read the words of Genesis 1:1: "In the beginning God created the heavens and the earth" (NIV). Both saw the same thing, but they had vastly different responses.

The question isn't whether God is present; it's whether we are aware of God all around us. St. Augustine wrote:

> Question the beauty of the earth,
> the beauty of the sea,
> the beauty of the wide air around you,
> the beauty of the sky;
> question the order of the stars,
> the sun whose brightness lights the days,
> the moon whose splendor softens the gloom of night;
> question the living creatures that move in the waters,
> that roam upon the earth,
> that fly through the air;
> the spirit that lies hidden,
> the matter that is manifest;
> the visible things that are ruled,
> the invisible things that rule them;
> question all these.
> They will answer you:

"Behold and see, we are beautiful."
Their beauty is their confession of God.[5]

When we relinquish expectations, we can move to acceptance and awareness of the God who doesn't reside in the box of our expectations but in all.

Mystical, Not Magical

Rex, the Floridian television mover; Karl, our kitesurfing instructor; and I sat on the white sand of the Gulf Coast during a kitesurfing lesson. Rex and I expected Karl to educate us on the intricacies of how we could use a massive kite to pull us across the water, but we also received wisdom on how to avoid any unwanted shark attacks. (For the record, I believe all shark attacks are unwanted.)

"I don't eat fish," Karl declared with no prompting.

I was curious, so I took the bait.

"Karl, why don't you eat fish?"

"I think sharks know that I don't eat their kind, so they will not try to eat me."

If there's even a small chance that his no-fish diet will arm him with better chances not to lose his um . . . arm, then more power to him. But we all know his "no fish eaten by me, therefore no shark will attack me" logic is completely ridiculous.

Psychologists would call this logic magical thinking. People with this logic believe that what we do has an unrealistic effect on the world around us. For example, some sports fans believe that the words spoken in a living room can jinx a team's fate on a field hundreds of miles away. The category in which magical thinking resides is populated by all other superstitious practices, like wearing the same pair of socks for every wrestling match to improve one's chances of victory.

Is believing that God is always with us also in the category of magical thinking? Believing that God is always with us kind of sounds like we have an invisible friend.

Magical thinking and mystical seeing are not the same. Those who practice magical thinking believe they are altering the world with their behavior. Mystical seeing doesn't change the world; it only changes how we experience it.

For example, in the Beatitudes, Jesus described an unlikely bunch as the ones being blessed: those who mourn, the meek, and the poor in spirit. Even though their world doesn't change, as they are still mourning and poor in spirit, nevertheless, they experience a blessing because they see the world differently.

This is what the best of the word *mystical* is calling us to: an ability to perceive something that isn't apparent to the senses or obvious to the intellect. Believing Jesus when he says that those who mourn are blessed or that it's better to give than to receive requires an ability to go beyond the material world, which disagrees with Jesus. We must be able to see as Jesus sees to embrace the mystery of God's omnipresence.

Magical thinking assumes that God equals good and therefore we need to do the right thing to cause God to show up and make all things good.

Mystical seeing is having a disposition toward the world that allows us to see the presence of the divine in all of it.

A few years ago my friend Pete Enns, who has a PhD in Old Testament from Harvard, was in the midst of a substantial professional struggle while his teenage daughter was going through her own struggle with an eating disorder. His daughter asked for a yellow Lance Armstrong Livestrong bracelet, which at the time was quite popular, before she went off to an institution for eating disorders.

Despite Pete's best efforts, he couldn't find one of those ubiquitous bracelets for his daughter. Everyone seemed to have one, but somehow Pete couldn't find one for his girl during this tough season.

Pete then went on a trip to Arizona to watch his son play baseball. While in Arizona, Pete and his son went to a barbecue with the baseball team. The party's host happened to be wearing a Livestrong bracelet.

Pete said, "Hey, you're wearing a Livestrong bracelet."

His host replied, "Do you want one? I have a garbage bag of them inside."[6]

Pete began to weep.

In that moment, Pete sensed that God was there because someone offered him a gift that he hadn't been able to give his daughter. To this day, Pete keeps one of the bracelets in his office as a reminder.

The story seems silly. It was just a cheap yellow bracelet, and Pete is seemingly too educated to think that receiving a yellow bracelet was anything more than a coincidence. But if you believe the world to be full of the glory of God, nothing is just a bracelet.

Those Who See God

Joan Chittister wrote:

> The great truth of early monastic spirituality, for instance, lies in the awareness that only when life is lived in the aura of the transcendent, in the discovery of the Spirit present to us in the commonplaces of life, where the paradoxes lie, can we possibly live life to its fullness, plumb life to its depths.[7]

I used to think Jesus's words "Blessed are the pure in heart, for they will see God" (Matt. 5:8) simply referred to the afterlife reward for those who were morally pure, specifically those who didn't drink beer or curse. But I no longer think that's what Jesus meant. This verse just might be about seeing God right here and right now.

Maybe those who see God are those who are not distracted by the worries of life, like our obsession with success, status, and popularity.

Maybe those who see God are those whose eyes haven't been polluted by their adamant demand for God to bend to their definition of good.

Maybe those who see God are those whose line of sight is unobstructed by their own constructed view of God.

The pure in heart don't need to wait to see God, because they have relinquished control over God and are open to accepting God right now.

4

Story, Not Answer

"The real question isn't if God will show up. The question is if we will be aware of how God has already shown up in all things. May those who have ears to hear, hear. Amen."

With those words, I finished the sermon.

I exited the stage as the music began to play, removed the mic from my face, and walked down the center aisle to my customary spot at the back of the sanctuary, where I greet people as they leave the service.

But one older gentleman couldn't wait the five minutes until the service's conclusion to share his thoughts with me. His walk toward me concluded half a step too late, my personal space now having two occupants.

"Luke, if God is everywhere, does that mean God is at a strip club?"

"Yes, but that doesn't mean I would make my lunch plans there," I said.

And now my personal space was back down to one occupant. The one who stayed was impressed with the clever retort. The other hasn't been seen at a church service since then.

Despite my flippant answer, I wholeheartedly understood his question. If God is everywhere, what about bad places?

Why his list of bad places jumped right past genocides and the Holocaust to strip clubs is an issue that I will leave to a therapist.

If God is everywhere, then what do we do about bad places?

I get the question, because the existence of bad always brings up questions.

Why Me?

Leading up to the 1994 Winter Olympics in Norway, the United States had two standout figure skaters, Nancy Kerrigan and Tonya Harding, who were vying to fill the top spot that had been vacated by the retirement of the 1992 Olympic gold medalist, Kristi Yamaguchi.

Nancy Kerrigan had earned the bronze medal at the 1992 Winter Olympics and had become a fan favorite, with endorsement deals with Campbell's Soup, Evian, Reebok, and Seiko.

Tonya Harding was arguably the more accomplished skater, having won the silver in the 1991 World Championships and being the first American woman to complete a triple axel in competition. But Harding never won the hearts of the American people and the big money endorsements.

On January 6, 1994, at practice before the US figure skating championships in Detroit, Kerrigan left the ice and walked through a corridor where a man hired by Harding's ex-husband struck Kerrigan above the right knee with a police baton, injuring Kerrigan to the degree that she was unable to compete in the US championship. Without a top spot at the US championships, Kerrigan would not be eligible to represent the United States in the Olympics.

Nearby cameras caught Kerrigan's immediate cries after the attack. "Why? Why me?" a teary-eyed Kerrigan screamed.

The existence of bad almost always brings up questions, for some almost instantaneously.

Love makes us promise. Two people falling in love will almost automatically make promises to each other like "I will love you forever" and "Till the day I die, I will be with you."

The existence of love makes us promise.

The existence of suffering makes us question.

In suffering, we cry, "Why me?" and "What did I do?" We see this in Jewish poetry.

> Why, O LORD, do you stand afar off?
> > Why do you hide yourself in times of trouble?
> > (Ps. 10:1)

And we see this in the Jewish prophets, like Habakkuk, who upon seeing his country's suffering said:

> How long, LORD, must I call for help,
> > but you do not listen?

Or cry out to you, "Violence!"
    but you do not save?
Why do you make me look at injustice?
    Why do you tolerate wrongdoing?
        (Hab. 1:2–3 NIV)

When our expectations for how we think life is supposed to go aren't met, we naturally question.

Where was God when the little girl got hit by a car?

Why does God make it so hard to understand God?

Why is the Bible so complicated?

Why is the church so imperfect?

We question if God is good.

My friend Betty lost her husband over fifty years ago, when she was in her late thirties and her two kids were young. In her grief, she questioned if God even loved her.

These questions of suffering have troubled humanity since the first family in Genesis.

Cain and Abel, the children of Adam and Eve, both brought an offering to God, but each received a different response from God. For reasons unimportant to the biblical writers, God appreciated Abel's offering but rejected Cain's offering. Cain couldn't deal with the suffering caused by coming in second place, so he killed his brother.[1]

In what many believe to be the last book written in the Hebrew Bible, Job wrestled with the question of how bad things could happen to a good person.

And just like in the sacred text, our question is, What do we do about suffering? If God is good, then there shouldn't be so much bad. This question makes us too rattled to sleep at night and too conflicted to sing during the day. It burrows through the mostly tightly packed barricade, because the best of answers cannot do justice to the worst of suffering.

We need something beyond an answer.

Better than an Answer

Speaking of suffering, let's talk about weddings.

It's an honor to perform wedding services. I love the mixture of nervous energy, naiveté, free food, love, debt, and the well-intentioned but often poorly executed jokes by the best man. It truly is a gift from the heavens to watch someone who has said to me, "Oh, you are a preacher; it must be nice to work only one day a week" fail at public speaking.

If you can strip away the pageantry, the nerves, and the cake, there is a miracle occurring in the service. Whether the couple is a pair of twenty-year-olds just beginning adulthood, forty-year-olds blending families together, or seventy-year-olds trying to find love again after burying their first love, a miracle takes place as two separate stories become one shared story.

To accentuate the integration of two stories into one, I ask the couple before the service to individually provide answers to the following questions about their soon-to-be spouse, which I then include in the wedding sermon.

What do you love most about the person you are about to marry?

What do you look forward to most about being married?

How would you describe your intended in five words?

How did you meet and what did you think about him/her initially?

Why did you choose to marry him/her?

I never thought those questions were that particularly difficult, nor did any of the couples I married.

Until I was performing the wedding of my friend Joel.

I met Joel my sophomore year in college when he was a high school sophomore who would come to campus to train with the college strength coach. After high school, he enrolled as a student at my college, which I suspect was so he could continue to use the weight room. Piece of evidence number one: Joel's groom's cake was made to look like a stack of weights.

After having the questions for weeks, Joel emailed me saying the questions were too hard for him to answer because he was a "simple guy."

As a side note, after Joel finished college, he went to med school at Tulane and then moved up to Boston, where he was the chief resident of orthopedic surgery at Harvard's teaching hospital, Mass General. Because, you know, Harvard lets a lot of "simple guys" become surgeons.

The next day I decided to make a call to Boston to help my simple surgeon friend. Just as I was about to call him, I received the following email from him.

Luke, you were there the day I had a life-changing decision, when I got the call from the scout and the next day when he wanted me on a plane to spring training but I told him no, I was more excited to go to medical school than play professional baseball.

Dr. Joel was drafted by the New York Mets after his senior year of college when he set a school record for home runs and was named an All-American. He got the call from the Mets while we were in the weight room working out. Joel walked over to the entrance to take the call, and less than five minutes later, he hung up the phone and walked back over to finish his workout.

I don't tell many people this, but after I turned down the New York Mets, I was so excited to go to Tulane. I packed my bags and went down to New Orleans, ready to start a brand-new adventure. I had a friend I had met at ACU. He had transferred for a year because of Hurricane Katrina. He was also starting medical school. We were going to be roommates. He told me that he already had a place and a room for me. I drive down, arrive, and what do I find and what does he tell me? "Sorry, bud, we don't have a room for you. The guy in your room isn't moving out, but we have a futon for you to sleep on if you want." A few weeks go by as I'm sleeping on a futon basically in a frat house. I am asking myself, What have I done? I just turned down the New York Mets. One morning my phone rings and wakes me up on the futon. I don't recognize the number. I answer, and it is one of the New York Mets' scouts and front office men. He says, "Joel, we want you and need you on the roster. What is it? How can you turn down your dream? Do you want more money?"

I told him that it wasn't the money and that I had made my decision. I am becoming a surgeon. I never asked what the second offer was. That day I told myself, I'm not giving up. I went and found an amazing condo in the French Quarter and moved off the futon. I also started my program that week, a combined MD, MPH program. In my first MPH class the first day, Katerina walks in, a bit late. She took my breath away. She was beautiful, exotic. We were introduced to each other by one of our friends, and I remember the date exactly: July 7, 2006. And that day she gave me a ride home, and I asked her if she wanted to grab something to eat one night. We did, and ever since then we have been best friends.

I thank God every day for her. I get asked often, "Do you regret turning down the Mets?" I can wholeheartedly say no. I would have never met Katerina. I didn't turn down my dream; I am living it.

Upon reading this, I had two thoughts:

1. I really hate myself. He's a better writer, athlete, and surgeon. Luckily, I can still dominate him in Bible trivia.
2. I hope my daughters find someone who would write a piece this beautiful about them.

I never got an answer to my questions from Joel, but I was okay without the answers, because Joel gave me something better than an answer.

Joel gave me a story.

Our prehistoric ancestors didn't sit around the campfire teaching their young about the world through lists of facts. The world was explained through stories, because they were storytelling creatures thousands of years ago, and we still are today.

Occasionally, someone will want to follow up with me after a sermon about a point I made or an interpretation of a text, but mostly people want to talk about a story I told that day or even weeks or months before, because we are storytelling creatures with a narrative hunger.

Even the most well-thought-out and polished answer can allow the water to leak in, because when it comes to making sense of suffering and injustice, answers always fall short. But stories can keep us afloat.

In his book *Unapologetic*, Francis Spufford put it this way:

> We don't say that God's in his Heaven and all's well with the world; not deep down. We say: all is not well with the world, but at least God is here in it, with us. We don't have an argument that solves the problem of the cruel world, but we have a story.[2]

Simple solutions sell, but in the end, simple solutions will almost always sell us short. Clichés about suffering roll off the tongue but don't sit well in the heart.

Maybe clichés work for some, but for the rest of us, they make it harder for us to keep our heads above water. Clichés weigh us down, but the Christian story can keep us afloat.

The Christian Story

According to the Christian story, God became a man—not a powerful, regal man, born in a castle with pomp and circumstance, but a peasant named Jesus, born to unwed teenagers in a small town and clothed in the shame and judgment that any child of questionable origin in a small, conservative, religious town knows. Jesus continued down the shameful path throughout his life, living with those on the outside of society while drawing animosity from those inside. Sorrow, loss, and betrayal were Jesus's regular experiences leading to his humiliating death.

God didn't step into the best and brightest areas of his created world. In Jesus, God stepped into darkness, into the absence of life and light, into pain and death. In Jesus, God was on the gallows, God was on the cross, God was in the tomb.

This story was so shocking that one of the first false teachings about Jesus was that he only appeared to look like a person. Jesus was fully divine but not fully human.

Because why would God step into such shame and darkness?

But this is our story. God is in the darkness with us. God doesn't stay removed from the world only to show up when things are good, like an absentee father returning after his kid hits it big and now has something to offer him. God isn't the old high school friend who comes out of the woodwork once they've seen the money we've accrued. God isn't a fair-weather fan pulling out the jersey when we make it to the play-offs.

God is the heavenly parent who stays by our side through all the tearful nights and heartbroken mornings. God is the constant consoling presence who is just as present in the struggle as in the victory. God is the loving spouse who holds our hand until the hospice nurse says, "It's time to say good-bye."

God doesn't "show up," because that implies God leaves. The only thing that ever changes is our awareness.

A God who exists within our suffering is a messy concept with plenty of unanswered questions. Straightforward and simple answers are preferable, but that's not life outside the garden. The great mystery of Immanuel, God with us, invites us into a complex and untidy existence. God might not speak or show up the way we want, but that doesn't mean God's presence isn't there.

In the story of the cross, God's willingness to enter into our darkest moments was fully displayed. The beauty of the Christian story is in God's willingness to become ugly. The beauty of the Light of the world is in God's willingness to go dark. The glory of the all-powerful God is in God's willingness to be weak.

Here's a section from what many believe to be the oldest part of the New Testament and the earliest song about Jesus. The earliest Christians understood Jesus's life as a story of God stepping into the worst of the human experience.

> Who, being in very nature God,
>   did not consider equality with God something to be
>   used to his own advantage;
> rather, he made himself nothing
>   by taking the very nature of a servant,
>   being made in human likeness.
> And being found in appearance as a man,
>   he humbled himself
>   by becoming obedient to death—even death on a
>   cross. (Phil. 2:6–8 NIV)

We don't have an answer for why there is suffering, but we do have a beautiful story of God being in the ugly with us.

For Me

For some who are processing adversity, the "everything happens for a reason" or "this was all part of God's plan" rationale helps them keep faith. And if that's you, I have no interest in trying to tear down what's keeping you afloat.

In her book *Learning to Walk in the Dark*, Barbara Brown Taylor encourages us to embrace darkness as a place to meet God. Conversely, she describes a type of faith, what she calls Full Solar Spirituality, that runs from the darkness.[3] To get her to rant against the evils of these Full Solar churches, I tossed her a softball question about them.

She didn't even take a swing at it.

"What is so wrong with Full Solar church?" asked the wise interviewer.

Taylor responded, "Nothing is wrong with it. I just didn't find it to speak to my whole life. Nothing is wrong with it. I often say to people, 'If it's working, why would you want to fix something that's not broken?'"[4]

I too don't want to be in the business of destroying something that works for someone else. Jesus said, "In this world you will have trouble" (John 16:33 NIV), and I don't want to be the type of person who adds to the trouble you are already going to have.

When I say answers don't work, I'm only describing what doesn't work for me and for many people I know; for some, the answers do help.

A family who attends a friend's church was driving home one evening when a drunk driver crashed into them, killing their child. This particular family found it helpful to believe that God had intentionally caused their child's death. They found solace in thinking that drunk drivers do not order the universe; God does.

For me, thinking that God causes the death of kids via drunk drivers is like charging purchases on a credit card because my bank account is empty. The problem is temporarily solved, but down the road a much bigger problem is waiting.

But it might work for them.

The word *good* is subjective, meaning I can't determine what a good answer is to you because your definition of good is different from mine.

While I don't have any interest in tearing down what's working for someone else, that doesn't mean their answer is true. Functionality doesn't equal veracity. Just because I hold to a certain tenet because it helps me doesn't mean it's true. The people who flew airplanes into the Twin Towers on 9/11 believed they were doing God's will, just as the KKK and Hitler believed they were doing God's will. And we can definitively say those three things were not true. Just because something is your truth doesn't mean it is *the* truth. That's not how the truth works.

But your truth still might help you.

While I don't have an interest in tearing down someone's answers, especially while they are experiencing grief, I am interested in helping those who have had their unrealistic expectations revealed to them and are now trying to find a way to keep their faith afloat.

That happens not just by getting a better answer but by acknowledging the limitations of all answers. Whether you are in the "everything happens for a reason" group or the "there's free will so bad things happen" group, there is still pain.

Even if God doesn't cause evil, God knows it is happening and doesn't do anything to stop it. God might not have caused the Ford Bronco to come around the corner while the little girl was walking onto the street, but God did not intervene either. Believing that God doesn't micromanage every painful detail doesn't make the divorce sting less or the rejection not hurt.

No answer removes all the pain created by tragedy.

Wrestling, Not Answering

Eugene Peterson said, "The world of religion, maybe more than any other, seeks to attract the 'terrible simplifiers.'"[5]

We like simple answers, but simple answers almost always sell us short in the end.

Healthy spirituality acknowledges the inability of simple answers to remove all tension from the hardest questions of life, but healthy spirituality doesn't walk away from wrestling with God. We can acknowledge the limitations of our ability to come up with an answer that ameliorates all anguish while still trying to gain insight.

At the heart of Judaism is an understanding that faith involves a strenuous engagement with the divine. The Jewish patriarch Jacob,[6] whose name in Hebrew means "heel grabber" or "deceiver," lived into this name by deceiving his brother and his father for a birthright and a blessing.

The night before Jacob came face-to-face with the big brother he had stolen the birthright and the blessing from years before, Jacob had a surprising encounter with God.

God didn't serenade Jacob with a sweet lullaby. God wrestled with Jacob.

And it wasn't a friendly wrestling match. God is so forceful that God permanently injured Jacob's hip, causing a lifetime of limping. But before the morning broke, God gave Jacob a new name, "Israel," which means "the one who wrestles with God." The Jewish people would take on Jacob's new name and be called the Israelites, meaning they are the people who grapple with God.

Anyone who says that engaging with God isn't a strenuous encounter is a deceiver. We all end up in moments like the one Jesus had when we ask for the cup of adversity to be removed, and, just like in the case of Jesus, the cup doesn't get removed.

We can't create an easy relationship with God, just as we can't eradicate all mystery or maintain all expectations.

Speaking of wrestling.

What I lack in handyman skills I make up for in networking skills. When my wife wanted to replace the carpet in our first home with a wood floor, I gathered a handful of guys from a Bible study to help me. The Bible study had hundreds of attendees, so I didn't know most of them, including a member of the Air Force named Ryan, whose roommate persuaded him to attend the workday at the Norsworthy home. Soon after arriving at my house and exchanging introductions, Ryan established himself as the project's alpha male through a combination of his skillful, Christlike carpentry and his loud grunting.

While Ryan was installing the new floor in my home, I noticed a USA Wrestling tattoo on his leg. I wrestled in high school, so we struck up a conversation about the sport. Ryan didn't say a whole lot about his wrestling prowess, but he did say that we should meet up at the Air Force wrestling room to roll. And since he helped (and by helped, I mean he did all the work) install my floor, the least I could do was join him for a workout on the Air Force base.

For background and to help with what's left of my self-esteem, let me inform you that I was an above-average high school wrestler in Ohio. I was by no means the best, but I had won enough matches to think I would be competitive with Ryan despite being fifteen pounds lighter.

I assumed incorrectly.

I didn't realize that Ryan was the Air Force's version of Hulk Hogan, having a high school record of 118 wins and 14 losses, a statistic he didn't share until after the mauling.

If you would like a video representation of what happened, you can google "lion attacks baby gazelle." I'm fairly sure whatever you find would be pretty close to what happened in that Air Force wrestling room.

There are some matches in which no matter what you bring to the table, you just aren't going to win. I tried to beat the Air Force Hulk Hogan for two hours and never came close. Jacob tried to outwrestle God, but for all his effort, he ended up on the losing side. I've tried to wrestle God into submission, and I too have never had a victory.

But something formative happens in the striving. The struggle of competition strips away veneers of hubris, revealing a level of honesty accessible only in exhaustion. When no breath remains to utter a platitude and no strength exists to posture, only the essentials persist. It's in that honesty and truthfulness that real connection with God flourishes.

When the whole family is in matching pastels for Easter Sunday, we rarely experience the story of death, burial, and resurrection. When we've been wearing the same wrinkled shirt for two days while staying in the ER waiting room, we can truly experience the power of Easter.

We might never get rid of the tension between a loving God and a world in which there is suffering, but we can find hope in the story of God entering into the suffering with us.

Limping but Blessed

Jason Jones and his three-year-old son, Jacob, drove home from church, while Jason's wife, Brea, and their two daughters stayed at church to prepare for their vacation Bible school. After Jason parked his Ford Expedition outside in the hot Texas summer sun, Jason and Jacob walked inside for nap time in their respective rooms.

A couple hours later, Jason woke up to a quiet house a short while before Brea and the girls returned. Upon arriving home, Brea went to check on Jacob in his room, but Jacob wasn't there.

Jason and Brea searched all around the house. Shouts of his name went unanswered. Panic set in.

Then Jason went outside and saw Jacob. His toddler body was passed out inside the Ford Expedition. Jason pulled his unresponsive son out of the hot vehicle and into the shade.

Brea called 911 as Jason began giving their son CPR, but nothing brought back Jacob's breath.

Jacob's time on earth concluded at three years.

Jason's book, *Limping but Blessed*, details his experience as a grieving father trying to make sense of his questions.[7] The "this was all part of God's plan" answer just made things worse for him, because that flippant answer made Jason feel that his son was expendable.

Jason, whose formal education was in finance, not theology, began searching for anything to make sense of the chaos, diving into the dense books most theology students read, such as those of the German theologian Jürgen Moltmann. Jason eventually sent Moltmann a letter with a litany of questions that arose during his grief—the hows, the whys, and the "What was God doing?" questions. Moltmann responded:

> We can find no answer to the why-question but we can survive with open wounds when we feel the presence of the suffering Christ who died with an open God question. In his passion we can also see the suffering of God and feel how God is bearing us. Behind the cross of Christ we see the morning of the resurrection dawning. The suffering with Christ gives us this hope.[8]

While we might prefer answers, and even expect answers, what we get is the story of a suffering God who enters into suffering with us.

Love Stoops

The Bible never explains why in an idyllic garden a tricky ser-
pent slithered around enticing Adam and Eve away from God's
utopia. We never get an exhaustive, straightforward expla-
nation describing why a force that pulls us away from God's
intention exists. Evil is simply understood as the background
for life. It's as if we all simply look at each other, shrug our
collective shoulders, and say, "Yep, that's the way it is." The
Bible doesn't do much to describe the why, but it does a lot
to describe the what now.

If the Bible were a movie, it would be a movie that thrusts the
audience into a world in which the hero has enemies at the
gates, but we know nothing of how they arrived or why they
are enemies.

When Jesus talked about people being blessed in the Beatitudes,
the notion of being blessed or happy was shocking to his original
audience. In the first century, people didn't want the gods to
see that they were happy, because they feared the gods would
punish them if they saw a human smile. Today we are the exact
opposite. If others don't see amazingly positive social media
status updates and if we don't answer every "How are you?"
with an "I'm great," there is a problem with us.

Our modern Western expectations cause suffering's persistence
to be a bigger question for us than it was when the biblical
stories were written. The biblical writers' concerns were less
about the presence of suffering, which they expected, and more
about how to respond to suffering.

But that doesn't mean I like it.

If I were Jesus's speech writer, I would cut the forgiving your enemies stuff and invest at least a few hundred words in the backstory for that devilish entity Jesus talked to in the wilderness. I would rather not have to forgive enemies in addition to facing the unanswered questions evil presents. But as it is, we must persist with a story of God stooping down in the person of Jesus and a God who continues to stoop down.

By the time my friend Ian was seventeen years old, he had already begun following in the footsteps of his alcoholic father, despite his disdain for his father's drinking. Ian had repeatedly begged God to make his father quit drinking, to no avail.

A friend forced Ian to step into an Episcopal church, despite Ian's lack of interest in God because of the unanswered pleas. Ian pouted through the service, thinking of how God had slighted him.

After the priest broke the bread for the Eucharist, Ian heard a voice that he described this way in his book *Jesus, My Father, and the CIA*:

> "Forgive me, Ian," it said.
>
> The voice was so close and real that I raised my head and looked to either side.
>
> "I'm sorry, Ian. Please forgive me," I heard the voice repeat.
>
> "Help me, I can't," I whispered.
>
> "Will you pardon me, Ian?" the voice repeated a third time.
>
> "Yes," I said.
>
> "Then we are both forgiven," the voice replied.[9]

Ian couldn't figure out this experience. He believed God was asking him for forgiveness, but that didn't make sense to him. As Ian went off to college and then later to seminary, the question continued to haunt him.

Was that voice the voice of God? And if so, can God ask for forgiveness from a boy?

Many years later Ian was in Denver at seminary when he met Miss Annie, a woman he described as the person whose lap was a revolving rest stop for three children during church. While at a church barbecue together, Ian asked her about his question:

> "Is it wrong for me to believe it was Jesus who asked for my forgiveness?" I asked.
>
> She frowned and shook her head. "Lord, what do they teach you at that School?" she said. Then she faced me head-on. "Did God humble himself by becoming a man?" she asked, every word spoken more loudly than the one before.
>
> "Yes ma'am—" I said. I'd never used the word ma'am before, but it seemed an excellent time to start.
>
> "Did he humble himself by dying on the cross to show us how much he loved us?" she asked, waving her spatula at me.
>
> My eyes widened and I nodded, yes.
>
> Miss Annie's body relaxed and she put her hand on her hip. "So why wouldn't Jesus humble himself and tell a boy he was sorry for letting him down if he knew it would heal his heart?"
>
> Ian replied, "But if Jesus is perfect—"

Miss Annie ambled the five to six feet that separated us and took my hand. "Son," she said, rubbing my knuckles with her thumb, "love always stoops."[10]

I can't say for sure if God apologizes, so if it turns out to be heretical to say that God apologizes to teenagers with daddy issues and drinking problems, please blame Ian, not me. But I know that for many, including people like the apostle Peter, the idea that God would humble himself to death, even death on a cross, was initially a heretical idea too.

I guess the reason Ian's mystical experience seems reasonable (or at least as reasonable as mystical experiences can be) is because the whole story of God becoming a person is about God stooping down to be with us in the most broken, vile, and subhuman part of our existence. And this is the story that the church has been singing about for two thousand years—the song of Jesus emptying himself, stooping low, and humbling himself to death on a cross.

Jesus stooped down not despite being God but because Jesus is God. In the incarnation, love stooped down. God chose to be vulnerable because that is the way of love.

Love offers forgiveness, and love receives forgiveness.

Part of marriage is having to apologize for what you did in your spouse's dream. I shouldn't be held responsible for how my wife's brain keeps her from being bored while she's asleep. I shouldn't have to be contrite because of the mixture of the random brain firings of her subconscious and some stupid, true crime story TV show that she watched before going to bed.

But nevertheless I find myself saying, "Lindsay, I'm sorry that in your dream I tried to fake my own death so that I could run off with my mom's best friend."

God is just as culpable for the expectations I place on God as I am for the dreams my wife has about me. But I think God has expressed love in bigger ways than my silly apology.

God becoming human and dying on a cross was God's apologetic expression of love. It was God's expression of nearness in our hurt. It was God's way of saying we aren't alone in our tears and we aren't forgotten even if we feel forsaken.

All Together

God is everywhere, or as Christian theology traditionally describes this attribute, God is omnipresent. But not everywhere is good. I wish I could jettison this tension, but those aren't the terms we are given in life.

Life is like a hospital elevator, where the highest of highs and the lowest of lows stand shoulder to shoulder. I once stood in an elevator in Dallas with a family that, based on my brief observations, was celebrating the birth of their first child. Mom sat in the wheelchair with her eyes fixed on the tiny human bundled up in blue, asleep in her arms. Dad stood behind her, arms weighed down with bags, blue balloon strings in hand, and pride pouring from his face. This was a moment they would never want to forget.

And there I stood bracing myself to be with a kid whose mother had been in a car accident. The paramedics had found her lying on the highway bloodied and bruised after being ejected from the vehicle. Her life would most likely be taken from her, making the kid I was preparing to meet an orphan.

One family braced to receive a new life, and the other family braced to lose a life. And that is human existence.

Life and death dancing together.

Gladness inhaled and grief exhaled.

And somehow God is the constant in all of it.

A few months ago I was in Nashville, Tennessee, about to preach the same sermon I preached at the beginning of this chapter. (I recycle sermons because doing so helps the environment. I'm not sure that's true, but it makes me feel better about repeating sermons.)

As I was about to deliver my environmentally friendly sermon, my phone vibrated. I'd received a text message from Pen Pal Paul. My daughter Avery calls him Pen Pal Paul because he lives in Australia and because Avery always appreciates appropriate alliteration.

Pen Pal Paul and I met where all good relationships begin: on the internet. In the years that I've known Pen Pal Paul, I have received only two types of text messages from him: a criticism of the state of American politics or a picture. And the thing about his pictures is they are always extremes. Thirty percent of the time the image is of a beautiful beach that he's sitting on, and the text says something like, "Texas doesn't have amazing beaches like we do here."

The other 70 percent of the time the picture is from his work as a producer/filmmaker with NGOs (or as we call them in

America, nonprofits) such as World Vision or Compassion International, for whom he goes to places like Syrian refugee camps or poverty-stricken parts of the developing world.

This evening as I'm about to preach the same sermon about God being everywhere, Pen Pal Paul sends the image of a mother with a two-year-old baby in her lap as the mother breaks rocks. For twelve hours of breaking rocks, she will earn two dollars.

Somehow I am supposed to believe and say that God is everywhere, even in a world that creates such disproportionate circumstances. My kids sit in the comfort of a middle-class life in Texas, and her kid sits in her lap while she breaks rocks. I don't have an answer for why, as Warren Buffett said, "fate's distribution of long straws is wildly capricious."[11]

But I do have a story of God stooping down into this unfair world and being a thread of hope for us to hold on to.

5

Character, Not Container

When I got married, I assumed I was just marrying the pretty nursing student who in bowling class once threw her bowling ball at me. But that's not how marriage works. You sign up to marry the nursing student who throws bowling balls at you, but then the whole family comes along as an added bonus (or in some cases, an added loss). It's like a few weeks after I bought my truck. I was trying to unlock the doors by pressing the unlock button on the key fob, and as I pressed the button for a few seconds, the windows rolled down miraculously. It was like that magnificent moment when Wonder Woman realizes that she can hit her forearms together and cause stuff to blow up.

Here's that three-layered analogy in a mathematical formula:

$$\frac{\text{Wonder Woman's}}{\text{arm things}} = \frac{\text{my truck's windows auto-}}{\text{matically rolling down}} = \frac{\text{me liking my}}{\text{in-laws}}$$

One of the more amazing in-laws I have is my wife's paternal grandfather, who goes by the name Bud. I'm fairly certain that's not his birth name, but I have never heard him called anything else. He's quite an amazing person: a veteran, a high school state champion in track, and the person who always wins when we play cards. But easily the best thing about Bud is the way he loves his family, including Shirley, his wife, with whom he spent sixty-one years before her passing a few years ago.

This past year when the family gathered for Christmas, Bud asked me to go with him alone to a back room because he wanted to ask me a question. I've learned that in these situations the questions are never about the best drill bit to use or how to replace a carburetor.

Yet again, I was right.

He said, "Drifter" (side note: he calls me Drifter, which I think is a reference to a pseudonym that Hank Williams used for a gospel album, but one can never be sure), "when I go to heaven, will I be able to see my grandkids and my great-grandkids, because I can't imagine being happy without them? And what's Shirley doing right now? Will I be able to recognize her?"

A question about carburetors would have been easier.

It's one thing to talk about heaven as an idea with an academic on a podcast; it's another thing to talk to someone for whom the great unknown isn't a great distance away.

In these moments, I feel an acute absence of adequate words. A brief homily on eschatology or an erudite exploration of the themes of the new heaven and the new earth isn't going to suffice.

I've read books that go into great detail, painting a picture of exactly what heaven will be like, describing the landscape of the backyard and the architecture of our homes. I get extremely curious about how someone can know the specifics about what our living quarters will be like in heaven. I've read the Bible, and I don't see that much specificity.

I've also read enough of the "I've died and now I'm alive again" genre to have my reservations. There has been one too many cases of fraud in that genre for me to want to put much stock in it. Maybe one day I'll come back from cynicism on this one, but for now, the whole genre gets a hard pass.

My suspicions about our current ability to predict the next act of God come from our predecessors' inability to predict the next act of God in their time.

If act 1 of God's redemption is God blessing the world through the Jewish people, then act 2 is Jesus and the church. Act 3 would then be the new heaven and the new earth.

People in act 1 were almost all terrible at predicting act 2. At the time of Jesus, hardly anyone really believed that Jesus was the next iteration. A run-of-the-mill reality TV star at the end of their fifteen minutes of fame has more followers than Jesus did at the end of his career.

If act 1, Judaism, couldn't predict with any success act 2, Jesus and the church, what makes me think I have act 3 figured out with the sparse available details?

All of that is to say, I have a hard time going into specifics about what the next life will be like.

I don't know exactly what our relationships will be like in heaven with our loved ones who passed before us or how we will relate to those who haven't passed yet. I've got ideas, but I'm not certain of any of them.

But I do hold one conviction: God is love.

So when Bud asked me what his relationship will be like with his wife of six decades who preceded him in death and if he will be able to see his grandkids and great-grandkids (i.e., my daughters), I talked about that one conviction.

"Bud, I really don't know the details of what heaven is going to be like. I don't know who you are going to recognize or how you can be happy without those you've preceded in death. I've got some ideas, but I don't know how good any of those ideas are. But my faith is in the belief that God is love.

"That thing inside you that makes you care so much for your wife and your family is love, which means it's godly, and maybe even somehow part of God. It might just be the image of God inside you. And I believe that God will honor that godly part of you and somehow make the whole thing right."

Whom Is God For?

The ability to be at peace with the unknown is based on trust. Faith isn't about having all the answers; it's about where we place our trust.

My middle daughter likes to do what she calls a "fall cuddle." It's one way that she uses my love and affection to delay her bedtime. To do a fall cuddle, she stands on the end of her bed with her back toward me, arms stretched out like a *T*, and then blindly falls toward me. She doesn't know when I will catch her, how long I will let her fall, what technique I will use to catch her, or how close to the ground she will be. The only thing she knows is that she can trust me.

If God isn't trustworthy, then we can't be at peace with falling into the unknown. The more trust we have, the more at peace we can be with the unknown.

For some of us, our inability to trust God in the unknown comes from our understanding of God. Perhaps God is more monstrous than trustworthy.

A few years ago, when I was living outside Dallas, I was meeting with a mentor named Mikel (pronounced "Michael"). As we were walking from his office to a favorite Mexican restaurant, he informed me that one of his employees got mugged while at one of his business interests in Colombia. I knew Mikel often went to Colombia, so I asked if he needed security with him while he was there.

Mikel responded in a manner similar to the way I respond when my middle daughter asks one of her five-year-old questions like, "Daddy, did you go to school when you were a kid?"

"Yes, Luke, I have security," Mikel responded.

"Like how many security people?" I said.

"Depends, but upward of a dozen security contractors."

It turns out that Colombia used to be pretty dangerous. I guess there had been a bit of a kerfuffle with drugs down in Colombia. But when this conversation took place, none of the now ubiquitous Pablo Escobar shows and movies were out yet, so how was I to know?

After lunch, he gave me a copy of the book *Killing Pablo*.[1] When your business is oil, you can have those kind of books in your office. If you are a pastor and you have a book titled *Killing Pablo* in your office, visitors become unnerved, especially if their name is Pablo.

Upon reading *Killing Pablo*, I was dumbfounded by the brazen corruption, violence, and darkness in Colombia around the time of Pablo Escobar. If you don't know about Escobar's reign of terror, you would also be amazed at the audacity and the scope of his crimes. Escobar started as a run-of-the-mill car thief and street thug, but through violence, street smarts, and the burgeoning cocaine business in Colombia, he became, at his zenith, Forbes's seventh richest person in the world.

Escobar's power found its mantra in the phrase *plata o plomo*, translated into English as "silver or lead." If you were on Escobar's side, you would receive extravagant amounts of "silver" in the form of money and rewards. Escobar's profuse generosity exceeded anything the Colombian government could offer Escobar's associates to turn on him. Escobar had lots of silver, and he gave it away generously to his friends, who ranged from common street thugs to powerful government workers, making his circle of friends almost as large as his bank account.

But if you weren't on Escobar's side, then you would get the lead. It didn't matter if you were a presidential candidate, a famous journalist, a police officer, or a judge. If you crossed Escobar, you could expect a visit from one of Escobar's ruthless *sicarios*. If you were one of the lucky victims, your death would happen quickly, but not every victim was lucky. It is rumored that

Escobar's preferred method of killing was by hanging his victims upside down and burning them alive. Escobar's seemingly endless generosity was only surpassed by his rampant violence.

Escobar purchased the support or the blind eye of policemen, politicians, and journalists not necessarily because of their greed but because of their fear. If you were a police officer, why would you want to be numbered among the estimated six hundred police officers who were killed by Escobar when you could stay alive and make thousands or in some cases millions of dollars by doing what many of your coworkers were also doing?

Escobar's ruthlessness made the choice to side with a drug lord easy, and it made him powerful, but it also made him a monster.

During the week when I was reading *Killing Pablo*, a pastor posted the following tweet: "Take Jesus as your Savior now before He becomes your Judge."

The way I understood that short sentence was that either we can accept Jesus as our Savior, who will give us a ticket into heaven, or Jesus will condemn us to burning in hell upon his return.

Accept Jesus's reward or face Jesus's punishment.

Heaven or hell.

Which sounds a lot like *plata o plomo*.

Escobar's victims at least found respite from their suffering in the grave. Jesus's lead lasts forever.

Almost everyone can conclude that Pablo Escobar's copious killings and gruesome violence made him a monster, so if God functions the same way, what does that make God?

Is God a monster?

If we live in fear of a monstrous God, then of course we can't trust the unknown.

I had a Colombian friend (not related to Pablo Escobar as far as I know) who, after I invited her to join us for a church service, said, "Oh, I couldn't do that, Luke."

"Why not?"

"Because of all that I've ever done, if I ever darkened the doors of your church, God would strike it down with a lightning bolt."[2]

A God who sends lightning bolts because of our shameful past sounds monstrous.

When God is a monster we can't trust to be around in this life, or one we can't depend on in the next, we need hard lines and clearly defined edges to make sure that we are on God's good side. When we don't know if God is for us, we have to protect ourselves in case God is against us. When we're in the hands of an angry God, we are always on edge, like the children of alcoholic parents. The uncertainty of how we will be treated creates perpetual anxiety.

Jesus Frees Us from the Monster

In Greek mythology, the greatest of the Greek heroes is the son of Zeus, Heracles (more commonly known by the Roman adaptation of the name, Hercules). Heracles crushed snakes as a baby, and as an adult, he slayed monsters like the nine-headed Hydra. The mythical Heracles freed the earth from the monsters that roamed the earth, causing many to believe that Heracles was a metaphor for the country of Greece. Heracles freed the earth from the monsters just as the great, enlightened civilization of Greece freed the earth from the precivilized monstrous ideas of human weaknesses and subordination to the deities.

In Christianity, Jesus is the one who performs the herculean task of destroying the idea of a monstrous God by showing that God is trustworthy, not a terrifying deity who strikes down sinners with lightning bolts.

The clearest picture of God is Jesus. As Scripture says, "All the fullness of the Deity lives in bodily form" (Col. 2:9 NIV). Or as Jesus himself said, "Whoever has seen me has seen the Father" (John 14:9). We must begin our understanding of God with Jesus, then let all other pictures of God be secondary pieces that give background and nuance.

We know that God isn't against sinful Colombians today, because Jesus wasn't against sinful Samaritans two thousand years ago. God isn't too holy to be around sinners now, because Jesus wasn't too holy to be around sinners back then. We see in Jesus that God doesn't choose the way of distant power but the way of intimate vulnerability.

Love always makes us vulnerable. If you never want to be hurt, then don't ever love someone.

I had a former CIA operative on my podcast, and so I needed a picture of him for my website. But the weirdest thing happened when I scoured online for a picture of him. I couldn't find a professional headshot. In fact, I couldn't find any pictures of him online at all.

When I asked him why his picture wasn't online, he said, "Luke, old habits die hard."

This is intro to 007 stuff, if you are a James Bond or a CIA operative (which in my mind is basically the same thing). You don't put pictures of yourself online, and you also don't get a significant other or kids. If you do, you definitely don't want to reveal them to anyone, because then you have a weak spot for an enemy to exploit.

Love makes us weak because love makes us vulnerable.

God doesn't display sovereignty by forcing people to worship but by relinquishing strength for the sake of others. God became a man named Jesus to display God's self-sacrificial love for humanity.

As Richard Rohr says, Jesus came not to change God's mind about us but to change our mind about God.[3] Jesus shows us that God isn't a monster to fear but a deity we can trust, so we can be at peace with mystery and the unknown.

The Love Is Big

My friend Tamara went down to an orphanage in Peru for a week with a group from our church. She has a gift for connecting with kids, whether they are American or Peruvian like Frank. Neither Tamara nor eleven-year-old Frank speak much of the other's language, but that didn't stop Frank from being by Tamara's side the entire week.

When it came time for Tamara to return to Texas, Frank was an emotional mess. As Frank hugged Tamara for the last time, with tears streaming down his face, he said in his rudimentary English, "The love is big."

I am reminded of the bigness of God's love, which Frank got a glimpse of through Tamara, when I see tattooed on her wrists the words "The love is big."

The answers might be small.

The light might be dim.

The certainty might be minuscule.

But the love, it is big.

Love is not a description of one of God's characteristics. Love is the essence of God.

Love is not a nice addition to our existence on earth; it is the center of our existence.

If God is the sustainer of the universe and God is love, then it is not gravity but divine love that keeps the whole thing together.

Like little Peruvian Frank clinging to Tamara, I hold on to my heavenly parent and acknowledge the essence of God, and I trust in the bigness of God's love even when I can't trust myself to understand everything else.

My conviction is that God isn't like a drunk, abusive father who needs to punish someone, and it's going to be us, until big brother Jesus appears to take our beating.

God isn't the fair-weather friend who loves us only when we are lovable.

God is love, and that love is big.

The love is not for our idealized self. The love is not for who we want to be. The love is not for the cleaned-up version of ourselves that we will become after six months of trying really hard. The love is not for the person we once were back before we went down the wrong path.

God's love is big enough for God to love who we really are. And God's love is big enough for us to hold on to when every belief and every certitude have slipped away from us.

Is God good in the sense that God lives up to every definition we have of what a good deity should be? No.

Is God good in the sense that God is benevolent and loving? Yes, and that's what I hold on to.

Green Boots

For two decades, John Aldridge and his childhood best friend, Anthony Sosinski, have made two overnight trips per week from Long Island into the Atlantic on their commercial fishing boat, the *Anna Mary*, but one trip can't be forgotten.

In the middle of the night with the boat on autopilot and Sosinski asleep down in the sleeping quarters, Aldridge needed to open the back hatch and fill up the holding tanks to get ready for the first lobsters they would be pulling onboard in a few hours. Two thirty-five-gallon ice chests sat on top of the filling tanks, preventing him from filling them. Aldridge pulled on a handle with enough force to move the two-hundred-pound cooler, but it was too much force for the handle.

The handle snapped.

The force needed to pull the two-hundred-pound cooler now propelled him toward the location of the back hatch he had just opened on the back of the boat.

Crashing into the water, he yelled, but his voice couldn't overcome the sound of the diesel engine or travel the forty miles back to the Long Island shore. Aldridge, alone in the middle of the Atlantic, thought this was going to be his end.

Sosinski woke up in the morning to find a broken cooler handle and an open hatch, but no Aldridge.

When Aldridge fell into the Atlantic forty miles off the Long Island coast in the middle of the night, his first thought was to shed layers by kicking off his boots, because everyone, fisherman or not, knows you can't swim wearing boots. But his green rubber boots, which had been weather tested for weather much harsher than Aldridge would ever experience in New York and thus were not usually worn by fishermen, were not pulling him under like the normal boots most fishermen wear would have. They were keeping him afloat.

The green insulated boots were buoyant, so he placed them under his armpits as two makeshift floaties. For almost eighteen hours, Aldridge stayed afloat until being rescued through a massive rescue mission by the Coast Guard and fishing boats, including Jimmy Buffet's boat, thanks to his green boots.

You can find a tattoo of those green boots on the arm of Aldridge's father, because he knows that his son is alive only because of those boots. The same boots that Aldridge's fishing buddies used to mock him for were his salvation.[4]

If you are a doubter or a skeptic like me, you don't need a complete understanding of every facet of faith. You just need a pair of boots to keep you afloat.

Many lose their faith because they structure their belief system in such a way that all the beliefs are of equal importance. When they get tossed into the water, they don't have the ability to reexamine any secondary beliefs that pull them under.

If their view of creation gets disrupted, the entire system can fall down. Or if someone shows them some of the contradictory stories in the Bible, they no longer think the Bible is inspired and God-breathed. If one chapter isn't historically true, then the other 1,188 chapters don't have any meaning. When they are pulled into the water and can't swim with every layer on, they end up drowning because taking off any layer isn't an option.

First Importance

Those who learn how to swim are those who learn the wisdom of first importance. Barbara Brown Taylor, in *Learning to Walk in the Dark*, describes how she used to have a metaphorical chest stuffed full of beliefs about God, but that's not the case anymore. "I cannot say for sure when my reliable ideas about God began to slip away, but the big chest I used to keep them in is smaller than a shoebox now."[5]

We can't swim while trying to hold on to a massive antique chest, but we can stay afloat with a small shoebox. What's in that shoebox may also keep us afloat.

Jesus and Paul both pushed toward this tiered level of beliefs.

Jesus prioritized loving God and loving people as being the most important. Paul also understood the importance of prioritizing beliefs when he told the church at Corinth, "What I received I passed on to you as of first importance" (1 Cor. 15:3 NIV). For me, the boots that keep me afloat are what Paul passed on as being "of first importance": "that Christ died for our sins according to the Scriptures, that he was buried, that he was raised on the third day according to the Scriptures" (v. 4 NIV).

Jesus, God in the flesh, the Messiah who fulfilled God's blessing of the world through the Jewish people (i.e., according to Scripture), was killed, buried, and three days later resurrected.

Nothing else is as significant as that.

Making sense of the texts of terror in which God's people commit horribly violent acts and the even more problematic ones in which God appears to be the one commanding those horrible acts to be committed is important, but it's not of first importance.

How God created the world is a big deal to many people because of the way in which science has been positioned as the enemy of faith, but based on how little creation is discussed in Scripture, how the world was created wasn't of first importance to the biblical writers. Only six times do the Jewish Scriptures mention God as the Creator of the world compared to over thirty times they reference God as the one who delivered Israel from Egyptian slavery. The creation references focus on who the creator was, not the process the creator used.

Even different ways of understanding the relationship between a loving God and a world that's full of hate and suffering doesn't make the list.

What I hold to is that there is no greater love than a person laying down their life, and that love is seen in God taking on flesh and dying for all humanity.

No Confirmations

My friend Lou sent me, his preacher, an email asking if his decision to get cremated would ruin his chances of getting into heaven.

I said no.

Am I sure about that?

Honestly, no.

I would be really disappointed if I was wrong about that. Not as disappointed as Lou would be, but still a little bummed.

But can I prove it? No.

Can I prove that the beliefs in my shoebox are true? No.

Can I remove every inkling of doubt and each modicum of skepticism that the resurrection happened? No.

To think that someone with an inquisitive mind can get all the questions down to a zero and empty out the mailbox of skepticism is unrealistic, which means there will always be a leap involved in faith.

The leap isn't just in the world of faith; it's also in the world of science.

In physics, string theory provides a unifying basis for many aspects of our universe by envisioning the most fundamental building blocks of all things as sub-sub-subatomic strings. To hold to string theory, one has to make a leap, because the strings can't be seen. Physicists believe that something exists, and the size is thought to be on the order of 10^{-35} m, but no one knows the shape or what the thing looks like, since, as I just said, it can't be seen.

We are certain that the strings are not visible in any normal sense of that word, yet physicists agree on string theory's truthfulness.

Something is believed to exist, and the something can be assigned properties that are consistent with and even help explain the behavior and characteristics of things that can be observed, but the something isn't actually seen.

I don't pretend to understand string theory, but I understand that to live is to leap because as humans, we are always under the inconvenience of our limitations. The question is where we will leap.[6]

Everyone must make a leap, whether it is toward or away from faith.

The leap might be toward resurrection or toward a reductionist view that there is only material human existence. Trusting in a material-only worldview is a leap too. It might be a smaller leap for some, but it's still a leap. Sam Harris, a neuroscientist and atheist, stated, "Any scientist must concede that we don't fully understand the universe."[7]

Some research will say that only 5 percent of the oceans have been explored. The oceans cover 71 percent of the earth's surface. Which means we haven't even explored a majority of the earth. So how can we say with certainty that there isn't a literal

God living in some crevice on the floor of the ocean with the Little Mermaid and King Triton?

Alvin Plantinga said that to say there must be a scientific cause for any apparently miraculous phenomenon is like insisting that your lost keys must be under the streetlight because that's the only place you can see.[8]

I'm not saying that the leap toward believing that God became a Jewish man who was raised from the dead isn't a bigger leap than believing that what we see, taste, and touch is all there is. The material-only leap might truly be a smaller leap for you than the leap of faith.

The issue isn't about the truthfulness of the Christian claims as much as it is about the ability to have knowledge. Most of the things in our lives that really matter can't be completely proven. I can prove that there are twelve eggs in a carton, and I can prove that my truck needs gas to run. But I can't prove what will always keep my girls safe at night. When my wife married me, she couldn't prove that I would be a loving and faithful partner.

We all make choices that shape who we become. For me, the choice I've made is based on the message of God becoming a peasant who died and then defeated death with love.

And that's a God I don't have to be afraid of. That's a God I can trust, even in the unknown.

Staying Afloat

Five months after my conversation with Bud about what heaven will be like, the family gathered for Mother's Day at the County

Line Barbecue joint in Austin. I was outside with our girls, and Lindsay was inside with twenty-plus people when Bud walked up to her with something on his mind.

"Hey, Bud, how are you?" Lindsay said.

"I'm good. I just wish Drifter would give me more specifics."

I too wish I had more specifics and less leaping, but until the day that faith becomes sight, I'll keep trusting that the details I have been given are enough to keep me afloat.

6

Dust and Divine

Let's talk about the popular Christian phrase "It's not a religion; it's a relationship." Let's begin by thinking about where this phrase gets communicated.

Usually, it's spoken in a building not required to pay property tax because it is deemed by the government to be a religious building. The mortgage for this non-property-taxed building is usually paid for with donations that are tax write-offs because the organization's founding members designated it a religious organization so that it qualifies as a 501(c)(3).

The person often saying these words probably receives a generous tax break because they identify as a religious leader.

Or maybe the phrase isn't said in a religious building but read in a book. If so, odds are that book was categorized as a

Religion/Christian Life book in the religion section of Amazon .com.

So maybe let's stop saying that.

That doesn't mean the critique is pointless. This critique—that religious functions can be mindless routines devoid of intimacy and honesty—comes originally from our religion's sacred text. Jewish prophets such as Isaiah and Hosea said that God doesn't want to endure heartless ceremonies, and to leave no ambiguity about God's feelings, the prophet Amos said that God hates those religious festivities.[1]

We all live in varying levels of obliviousness to our surroundings, creating varying degrees of self-contradiction. A friend from seminary, Mark, the most outspoken pacifist I knew at that time, was also in more fistfights than all of my other seminary friends combined. Not many seminary students get in fights, so that's not saying much. But this next story might give a better illustration. Mark, while teaching the university's football players martial arts in an off-season team workout, beat up a football player who was fifty pounds heavier than him after Mark saw the player hitting a smaller football player too hard.

Like the pugilistic pacifist, I too am self-contradicting. A long-time workout partner once told me that while listening to me preach, he thought, *Luke should really listen to himself.*

With the understanding that we are all self-contradictory to some degree, let's go back to the "relationship not religion" issue.

It takes a very generous massaging of the English language to say that a relationship with Jesus isn't done in the context of religion. The sacred text we read, which gives us most of our understanding of Jesus, wasn't an email we received directly. The Bible is a collection of stories, sayings, songs, and speeches compiled by the church over hundreds of years until it became the book we have today.

The stories we tell about Jesus speak not just to the person of Jesus but also to all who have followed him over the last two thousand years. Jesus cannot be removed from his position as the central figure in the world's largest religion, a newsworthy position in the world's second-largest religion (Islam), and a participant in the fifth-largest religion (Judaism).

But I get why we make the idealistic and naive statement about having the option to choose Jesus over religion. It's the same rationale for why I don't eat pizza crust or read introductions to books. We want to discard the bad and keep the good.

If the "relationship not religion" move actually worked, we wouldn't have to worry about the church's sex scandals or the Crusades. We could pretend that those who used our sacred text in support of slavery and inequality aren't connected to us. We could laugh off the money-hungry televangelist, and we wouldn't have to treat those Christians who picket funerals like that shady uncle we keep our children away from at family reunions.

If only it were that easy.

The "I have a relationship, not a religion" idea comes from the same impulse that makes people ask, "If God is everywhere, then is God also at strip clubs?" God and, vicariously, God's people are supposed to be good, but the reality doesn't match our definition of what good is supposed to look like.

If religion doesn't look like it's supposed to look, then we will opt out. But there is another option.

The rough edges might be the very place where we can honestly connect.

Human Hand

When I was in grad school, I did a little personal training as a side job. I had a friend and client named David, a successful antiques salesman, interior decorator, and smoker.

Often, he would complete a running workout on the track, and before he had even gotten to his Cadillac in the parking lot, he would light up a cigarette. This always made me wonder where he was hiding the cigarettes during the workout. Early on I knew that David wasn't going to win any marathons, but I got a little work and he burned some calories and Marlboros, making both of us happy with the arrangement.

On occasion I would help him with other projects. One time I was helping David with an installation in a customer's home, which is a nice way of saying I was carrying in really expensive furniture. Having just purchased a bookshelf for my home from Target, I was particularly curious about the extremely heavy wooden bookshelf that I carried. Usually, I didn't care about the price of fine furniture, since only people in a tax bracket I will never inhabit could afford it, but alas I asked the question.

"How much is this shelf?"

"Five."

"Five hundred?"

"No. Thousand."

Having just spent thirty dollars on my bookshelf, I didn't see with my uneducated eye why someone would pay that much for a bookshelf. The piece actually looked inferior to the perfection of my composite wood bookshelf.

My bookshelf's straight lines and perfect symmetry showed no sign of error or variation in the manufactured grain.

The wood on his shelf was a strange mix of chaos. The grains danced unpredictably. The wood's character wouldn't submit to any craftsman, and the skilled carpenter didn't try.

Seeing my confusion, David explained that his "qualified buyers" value one thing a piece like mine would never have: the work of a human hand.

For those who have eyes to see, an overly processed shelf lacks humanity and honesty, because it's not a real piece of wood. It's composite wood, which is a nice way of saying it's glued together sawdust. A manufactured piece of wood can be made to submit to our expectations of perfection because it's our own creation, but a piece of oak mocks our attempts. The stubbornness of real wood is the most valuable part, because that's the most honest part. No matter how hard we try, it will be what it is, not what we will it to be.

In the second creation story, God took the dust of the ground (in Hebrew, the word is *adama*) and breathed into it the divine breath, creating the first man, named Adam, which is the generic Hebrew word for "man."

We are the dust from the ground infused with the divinity from above.

We are a mixture of dust and divine.

Attempts to distance us from the dust divorce us from ourselves. Our airbrushing of ourselves on social media and every deceptive utterance of "Oh yeah, I'm doing good" strip us of our God-given duality, turning us into composite characters.

We are not filtered and "Oh yeah, I'm doing good" creatures.

We are both broken and beautiful.

To the trained eye, our honest humanity can become the most valuable thing we have to offer, because that's what unites all of us. No one has ever connected with someone because they have a perfect life, a perfect spouse, a perfect bank account, and 2.5 kids in matching clothes on the lawn of their cookie-cutter suburban home next to an SUV adorned with a 13.1 bumper sticker.

When someone's life is perceived (and don't for one second think it's anything other than a perception) as too smooth, there's nothing for us to grasp.

The rough edges give us a grip to hold.

We don't need to run from the edges, the imperfections, the unfiltered, as we've done far too often in the religious world.

Church on Fire

One Sunday morning our family sat together for a service, my parents bookending my eight-year-old redheaded brother and me. His ginger locks and the green pews usually made for a festive spirit year round, but this Sunday wasn't so holly or jolly, as our church was meeting in a temporary location because our normal building was out of commission.

With a quickened pace and heavy breathing, the preacher, holding up a church bulletin, approached my father. The bulletin's cover image, as always, was a picture of the church's building, a design choice that still seems odd. But on this particular bulletin, which was held high enough for all to see, the image of the building had been defaced by someone's pencil. Usually a doodled-upon bulletin doesn't garner any attention, but since our church building had burned down just weeks before, the preacher had a right to be a bit on edge. Suspicions of arson were wafting in the air, but no one had been charged at that point.

When the preacher saw a bulletin that had been altered to show the building on fire, he thought he would put his Sherlock Holmes's hat on and see if this was a clue to the arsonist's identity. My father is a psychologist, but he's not a CSI psychologist, though that didn't deter the preacher from asking if my father could deduce anything about the artist.

"The picture was drawn by a young boy. Probably around seven years old. Definitely left-handed," my father said.

"Really? You can tell all that from the picture?" the investigative preacher said.

"No. I can't tell that from the picture. I can tell you that because I saw my son Luke drawing it."

The crestfallen preacher didn't find where the fire began, but at least we see where my inappropriate sense of humor began.

Our next church was burned by a preacher who went to jail for sexual contact with a teenager.

Six months into my first full-time job, all the elders resigned after a nonsexual incident involving a child from church and one of the elders.

People get burned in churches all the time. The white, conservative church during slavery, segregation, and the civil rights movement was at best silent, most likely complicit, and at worst explicitly supportive of the heinous sins of racism and slavery. An overwhelming number of private Christian schools in the United States began around 1970, which was just after the time of the Little Rock Nine and the integration of schools. For many, private religious schools became a pretext for fleeing from integration.

Is it any wonder that people play the linguistic gymnastics of saying they aren't religious but in a relationship? It's the same reason why Gandhi famously said he likes the Christ but not the Christians.

I'm Part of the Problem

Once a church lady expressed, with a hint of moral superiority, that her kids didn't like church because they thought church was hypocritical. Her accusatory tone made clear that this was an issue for the professional Christians to fix. What she couldn't see was whom the accusation was most directed toward. Her kids' closest connection to Christianity wasn't a preacher.

It was her.

She wanted to blame others for her kids' lack of appreciation of church without acknowledging that to some extent their critique of church was a critique of her.

The issue with the church isn't just out there; the issue is within me. I have to own up to my complicit and explicit participation in the behavior that distances people from religion.

I can bemoan the racism of the church, but can I acknowledge the way I value my privilege and the subconscious biases that reside in my heart?

I can call out the violence of the Crusades, but will I examine the way I've used power to get my way?

I can call out materialism in the church, but will I examine the way I've intentionally or unintentionally sided with those with influence and money?

I can complain about how the church has burned people, but will I own up to the ways I've overworked overly eager members to the point that they are burned out, causing them to feel that the church only cares about what they can do for the institution's maintenance and growth instead of caring for them as a person?

People don't live up to who they claim to be. This isn't just a church issue; it's a human issue.

Pacifists get into fights.

Health nuts eat at Cinnabon.

In moments of weakness, atheists backslide into prayer.

As Scripture says, the good we want to do isn't what we end up doing.[2]

When calcified into organizations, these issues are heightened in their scope and their scale. Institutions, whether explicitly religious or only subtly religious (like sports, politics, or business), will always have cases in which the dust is magnified at the expense of the divinity. And unless we get rid of all connection and interaction between people, there will always be perverted forms of community that hurt people. This doesn't excuse the evils of organizations, but we also shouldn't scapegoat institutions and excuse ourselves.

Still, the presence of sin doesn't diminish the presence of beauty.

Community of Robbers

Jason Micheli, a foul-mouthed Methodist pastor with his own cynicism issues, wrote a good-looking book called *Cancer Is Funny* in which he talks about his battle with cancer. According to his doctors, Jason's form of cancer is one that he will wrestle with for as long as he's alive. For a critical thinker with a fair share of cynicism, this would concurrently be a diagnosis for rampant cynicism.

But his cynicism hasn't spread; it has actually shrunk, because of the church. Or as he put it, "Community robbed me of my cynicism."[3]

The church has flaws because the church is made up of people. And when those people are given time and power, those flaws can show up in real ways that can cause real pain. If you've experienced them, I would never want to diminish or dismiss your hurt. There are far too many people with far too many legitimate reasons to never want to participate in the church ever again because of terrible experiences with the church.

But I think many of us continue to show up in churches, in all their various forms, through all the years, despite all the scandals, despite all the burns, because there is a cynicism-stealing divinity when people gather around the life-giving gifts of grace the church has to offer.

When I stood next to a mom and dad whose hearts were broken because of their son's suicide, yet they continued to sing through their grief and their questions, it was hard for me to think that any of my issues were substantial enough for me to stop singing.

When I sat with a Congolese friend who, while he was a college student, experienced a genocide breakout in his country, fled to a refugee camp in another country, was separated from his parents without any way of knowing where they were or if they were even alive, and was able to say, "God is always good," it was hard for me to think of reasons why I couldn't sing about the goodness of God.

When a church member mails a check to cover a month's mortgage when you can't sell your home back in Florida or when a church rallies around a family that's been torn apart by one partner's addiction or when a church becomes the adopted family to an isolated single person, the divine isn't hard to find.

There's an old Buddhist story about a mother who lost her child. She asked the village's holy man what she could do to get rid of her grief. The holy man told her to find a mustard seed from a home that hadn't been touched with loss. So the grieving mother went from home to home in her village asking if they'd been touched by loss.

One home after another, each family shared the story of the loss they had experienced. Home after home, the woman walked away with no mustard seed. She never received what she was looking for, but she did receive what she needed:

stories of fellow travelers on the road of grief. What saved her wasn't a magic seed but the divinity of people sharing their humanity.[4]

The divinity of the church can rob us of our cynicism, not because everyone asks the same questions or travels the same road but because community embodies divinity for us in suffering.

Go Fast, Go Alone . . .

An old African proverb says, "If you want to go fast, go alone. If you want to go far, go together."

The dust of community might slow us down, or even bring us to a screeching halt, but it can also give us endurance for the long run.

One morning at the gym I saw a trainer with tears in her eyes. She told me she had just received a phone call from her next client, who had to cancel her appointment because her son had committed suicide. Her son was eleven.

The divinity of community is that in a moment like that, when most people don't even know whom to call, I know exactly whom to call. I know the people who have tasted that type of suffering and have found a way to keep on going.

I once sat on the back porch with grieving parents whose child had died just hours before and heard these words from the father: "God is amazing, because I see God's love in all of these people."

If that doesn't rob you of your cynicism, I don't know what will.

A Community of Beholders

The beauty of this community has been stealing cynicism and skepticism for two thousand years. We don't have to look too hard to see the sins of the church, but the church is also a living testimony to the beauty of God, which has given life to billions of people.

I used to assume that Constantine's conversion in the fourth century was the cataclysmic event that changed the church by bringing Christianity to the mainstream, but that's not what historians now tell us. Christianity didn't become strong because of the emperor's conversion. Instead, Christianity's strength caused the emperor to convert. The millions of Christians making up Constantine's empire gave good reason for the politician to join the church. In much the same way, some American politicians align themselves with Christianity regardless of the authenticity of their own faith for the sake of the Christian vote. By the fourth century, Christianity's beauty was already changing the world, even before the conversion of the world's most powerful person.

Julian the Apostate was the emperor two decades after Constantine, and as his name indicates, Julian the Apostate was not a Christian. His attempt to move Rome back toward the paganism that had existed before Constantine struggled because of the beauty of Christianity. Here is what Julian the Apostate said about his difficulty eradicating Christianity. (Note: Julian the Apostate called Christians "Galileans" because of Jesus's hometown or "atheists" since Christians didn't worship other gods.)

> Why do we not observe that it is their benevolence to strangers, their care for the graves of the dead, and the pretended

holiness of their lives that have done most to increase atheism. For it is disgraceful that, when no Jew ever has to beg,
and the impious Galileans support not only their own poor
but ours as well, all men see that our people lack aid from
us. Teach those of the Hellenic faith to contribute to public
service of this sort.[5]

The Jesus movement's beauty captured the attention of the
world because Jesus followers cared for orphaned children,
the abandoned sick, and the dead. Christians, like their name-
sake, cared for people on the margins and sacrificed themselves
for the sake of others. Christianity was the cataclysmic event
that said that all people—even those who are different from
you—matter.

The Nondenominational Game

A somewhat popular fad in the church these days is for churches
to drop the denominational affiliation from their names. I did
this when I named the church I started, and it had the effect
I was looking for.

Dozens of times I had this conversation in my church-planting
days:

"What do you do?"

"I'm starting a church."

"What kind of church is it?"

"Nondenominational."

"Oh, that's great. We like the nondenominational churches."

Our culture's zeitgeist is heavy on distrust and disdain for institutions, whether they be big business, government, or church. So naturally, the average person would rather be distanced from a denomination. But this disdain is not just an in-vogue preference of nonchurch people; it's also the church's fault. The sins of our predecessors and our own sins have caused the disdain for denominations. By dropping a denominational name, churches can appear to separate themselves from racism, legalism, judgmentalism, and other closeted skeletons.

Making visitors feel more welcome in church, and therefore more likely to experience the love of God, is a good reason to change a name. This is a very small step for a church to take that could make a substantial difference in someone's life.

But at the same time, there is a good reason for churches to keep their denominational names. If we keep the name, it helps us to be honest about who we are and where we came from. It makes us acknowledge that we have sins in our past that we can't sweep under the rug.

If Baptists keep the words "Southern Baptist" on their signs, hopefully at some point they will acknowledge the unsavory history their church had with slavery and racism, which caused the creation of a separate group of Baptists.

I keep saying I'm from the Churches of Christ, and almost every time I do, I have to apologize for how my denomination, in the height of its hubris, said we were the only Christians going to heaven.

A denominational name is a small way to help us acknowledge the dusty elements from which we came. We can't pretend they don't exist because they are part of our past and who we are in the present.

But we also don't have to stay in those sins. We can move into new levels of maturity.[6]

Stand-Up

After interviewing comedian Pete Holmes, I was driving him and the comedian who opened for him, Brent Sullivan, from the theater to their hotel in Dallas in the wee hours of the morning. The conversation veered into my perpetual interest in stand-up comedy. One of them asked if I had ever thought of trying it, to which I quickly said no.

I hadn't even been to a comedy club before, let alone tried to get on the stage, but in that moment, the stand-up virus was passed on to me, and it began an almost yearlong process of wearing down my antibodies. Specifically, the antibodies it wore down were my self-respect and dignity.

I usually take July off from preaching for a study break and vacation. But the July after the infection began I used my July to try stand-up a half dozen times. So here's my story of trying stand-up comedy.

The first open mic was in a sparsely populated bar. Maybe a dozen people were in a room that easily could have fit a hundred. Knowing enough about room dynamics, I knew this crowd in that room would feel dead and cold even if every person was laughing uncontrollably, so I didn't gauge the success of the night on anything other than my ability to avoid falling down or crying while on stage.

A week later I went to a different venue in downtown Austin. There was a much better crowd, but the venue was outdoors.

In July. In Texas.

I was at the end of the list and knew the crowd couldn't survive that long outdoors. By the time I got up, the venue was basically empty, and again I couldn't get a genuine feel for how my set went.

So I was two times in with no real ability to assess how well I had done.

The third time was the charm.

Well, not really.

I was scheduled for a set at one of the two best comedy clubs in Austin, so I knew the crowd was going to be good. I arrived at this club on Sixth Street, the heart of Austin's night life, thirty minutes before the open mic began, and my nerves started firing like I was back in high school before a championship match in a wrestling tournament. The irony was I was doing a four-minute set in front of forty people when each weekend I do multiple thirty-minute sets for a thousand people, and I never feel this way.

My set mostly consisted of the best stories I tell in sermons— the ones I've used in multiple venues in multiple states all with solid responses, like the fake-teeth story.

I told the first story, and I didn't even get a courtesy laugh. I started to feel warm and a bit sweaty.

The second story . . . again, nothing.

At this point, the room felt about 119 degrees and I wanted to get out.

When you tell an unfunny joke in a sermon, usually you stop trying to be funny and move on to something serious. When you tell an unfunny story in stand-up, you don't get to transition out of humor. Instead, you have to keep on trying to be funny, all the while every unfunny joke makes the next joke even less funny. Stand-up is mostly about confidence, and when it's gone, it's gone.

After the second unfunny story, I had the confidence of a pimple-faced freshman trying to find a date for the homecoming dance.

Comedy clubs flash a light at the back of the room when you have one minute remaining. When I heard the light come on (yes, I actually heard the light come on; like I said, it wasn't going well), it was a lighthouse of salvation putting me out of my misery.

I left the stage and slouched into a seat. While I waited until I could slip out the door without looking as if I was running home to my mommy, the next guy did a set about toaster ovens, and the room loved it.

Nothing makes you feel like a failure more than Pop-Tarts puns working better than your stories.

I drove home debating how I could end my July break from preaching early so I could feel like I had some proficiency with public speaking again. I arrived home and sent Brent an email with the subject line "Self-Esteem Destroyed."

Here's the conversation.

Brent,

I did two open mics at crappy venues in the past week, which didn't get me a fair read on my stand-up attempt. I did my third at a good venue, and it was awful. I haven't felt that bad after talking in front of people in over a decade. So just FYI—next time you are asked to preach a sermon, the jokes that work in church are not the same jokes that work at a comedy club.

Luke,

Hahaha I'm sorry to hear it, man. If it makes you feel any better, you just described about all of my open mic attempts in the first year. Open micers are allowed to suck. Plus as a minister you have the fundamentals of a great performer. It'll click sooner rather than later.

Brent,

Because of your help I'll do what I can to put a good word in with God if it turns out when I die that my whole life wasn't based on a lie.

Luke,

Hahaha thank you! That should be your opener next week at the mic. Break a leg.

I usually don't like to mention in initial conversations that I'm a preacher because when people find out, their openness and honesty evaporate. So of course I wouldn't say anything about being a pastor in a set at a comedy club. Brent's suggestion for my opening joke made me think that hiding my occupation was maybe the exact opposite of what I was supposed to do.

I soon got an email from the other prominent Austin comedy club that I had been trying to get into all month, saying that I was booked to do a set in three nights. I didn't want to get up on stage again after my jokes had been toasted.

See, toaster puns are the worst.

I would have rather done a 5 a.m. men's Bible study on Leviticus than suffer through another failed attempt at comedy, but something in Brent's email made me accept the offer and do a whole new set, not with my preacher stories but about being a preacher—the very opposite of what I had done before. Instead of running away from my humanity, I leaned into it.

I leaned into the struggles I have by not only placing my faith in something I can't prove but also investing my career and my ability to provide for my family in something that can't be proven with a scientific test.

I leaned into the struggles I have with the church's reputation for being hateful to the LGBTQ community.

I leaned into the judgmental reputation that we in the church have earned.

And the weirdest thing happened in this next set. It actually worked.

I said things, and the crowd responded with laughter. Like a pimple-faced ninth grader walking tall after getting a date with the prettiest girl, I grew in confidence. I kept telling jokes, and they kept on laughing.

Almost all my jokes landed, and I even said something positive about God in a venue where such a thing is hardly ever said.

And I didn't even have to make a stupid toaster joke.

Connection

I've done the same set a few more times since then, and it's consistently gone well. I'm not quitting my day job, but it has gotten laughs each time. It's impossible to say exactly why jokes about being a preacher work, but I guess they work because there's something relatable about leaning into the complexity of humanity. Not pretending it doesn't exist. Not creating linguistic gymnastic routines to make it look as if we aren't complicit in the problems.

Whether we have the vulnerability to discuss such things or not, we all know that we have unresolved issues, shameful memories, and self-contradictions residing in us, and those collective experiences can connect us. Our rough edges give others an ability to connect and hold on to us, and others' rough edges allow us to connect with others. When someone's life is perceived as too perfect, we have no ability to connect.

Our humanity, with all its flaws and contradictions, can be the very thing that unites us. This isn't to say that the terrible atrocities of racism or abuse need to be dismissed as "people just being people." Those sins need to be dealt with, and the church needs to repent of the way it has too often sided with the powerful victimizer over the victim.

But it doesn't have to end there.

The popular saying that the church is full of hypocrites isn't true. The church isn't full of hypocrites. There's always room for another. Because that's what we all are.

When we own up to the ways we have displayed our dust through the power of confession and honesty, we can see our shared need for grace.

When we acknowledge that the line between good and evil doesn't run between us and them but down the middle of us all, our shared need for redemption can bring us together and enable us to move into new phases of maturity.

Second Half

The religious tradition I grew up in is a young tradition, not much older than a hundred years. We've displayed our lack of maturity by our adolescent ways. In the darkest corner of my tradition, some voices still declare that we are the only ones going to heaven. The egocentrism of my tradition must be heartbreaking to our heavenly parent. Few things that someone could say to my children are worse than telling them that their father doesn't love them or accept them. And that's pretty close to what my tradition has said to the other children of our heavenly parent when we've said that we are the only true church that God loves and accepts.

This is what the Franciscan priest Fr. Richard Rohr calls "first half of life" thinking.[7] In the first half of life, we strive to find our place in the world, often by differentiating ourselves from those around us. This is the adolescent playground behavior of seeing which kid is the fastest or the prettiest that some of us never outgrow. We just replace speed and good looks with finances and success.

In the second half of life, we stop trying to separate ourselves from others and instead focus on the commonality that brings us all together.

One benefit of having doubts is an awareness that we are all simply doing our best with the unwieldy task of making sense of God and this world. We acknowledge that our best isn't impervious to error or even to sin. Hopefully, we can then extend grace to others by believing that they too are doing their best to make sense of God and this world.

When we find ourselves washed out to sea and simply doing our best to stay afloat, we have a chance to develop a more generous and inclusive attitude toward others. When used correctly, doubts can limit the cocksure certitude that puffs us up and replace it with a love that builds up and builds together.

All good theology teaches us to love the people in front of us, which includes those who come from different traditions and those with different convictions than our own, because we realize we are all in this together.

For the sake of honesty, let me tell you one group of people I struggle to love: people on airplanes wearing medical masks. To be clear, if people are actually sick or have an autoimmune issue, my problem is not with them. My issue is with perfectly healthy people wearing masks.

Planes are basically flying petri dishes. I say that as someone writing these words while flying over the Atlantic Ocean wrapped in two blankets, which no doubt contain the dead skin and living germs of a previous passenger.

But medical-mask people, it's not fair for you to try to get out of this mile-high germ swap. Don't pretend like you are somehow exempt from this virus exchange program known as flying. When you choose to fly, you sign up for the modern miracle of being in the air like a bird and catching a cold. That's the deal.

If I ever get arrested, most likely it will be because I've gone up to a fellow traveler wearing a mask, ripped the mask off their face, and then whispered ever so gently in their ear, "We are all in this together."

Because we are.

We are all in this world together.

We have one good world entrusted to our care, and we have to do this thing together.

After I did my month of stand-up comedy, the weirdest thing happened. People heard about my preacher routine and started sending me their own jokes. And some of the jokes were actually funny. Not all, but some.

The jokes ranged from church as the largest pyramid scheme to the ridiculousness of believing crackers can become the body of God incarnate to how terrible religious people can act.

These jokes were not sent in by people who didn't financially support a church or didn't believe in the sacraments or didn't serve their faith communities. They were people of deep faith who were committed to their churches financially, were shaped by the church's sacraments, and served in their local churches.

I think these jokes came in because people wanted the catharsis of acknowledging their struggles. When we have only a binary lens of faith or doubt, pressure builds up with no release valve because our only options are giving up on faith or suppressing our doubts, and neither of those options is a prescription for healthy spirituality.

When we stop focusing on just the dust and the differences, we can see in others the divine. When flaws don't limit someone's ability to have strengths in other areas, we can reap the benefits of how they function in the body of Christ. When we have an awareness of the complexity of the task of theology and the differences other faithful women and men have had throughout church history, we don't jettison our brothers and sisters because they, like others, have made choices different from ours.

We experience new layers of God's character that different parts of the body of Christ best reveal. When the question isn't "Do they do everything right, and by right I mean my way?" but instead "What can I learn from them?" we can grow.

The message of the church is that we are all in this together with all our flaws and all our humanity. When we mature past the immature games of differentiating ourselves from others based on petty minutia and instead work toward unity, we can give grace to those who have been burned by the church and hopefully earn back their trust.

A BIBLICAL INTERLUDE

Now a few words on the book the mysterious writer of Hebrews described as living, sharper than any two-edged sword, able to divide soul from spirit and to judge the intentions and thoughts of the heart.[1]

Bay Bible

My early view of the Bible had lots of explosive moments, overly airbrushed characters, and not much humanity. I had basically turned the Bible into a Michael Bay movie.

I believed the Bible to have been created through some sort of Star Trekian light from heaven, causing the biblical writers to go into a trancelike state and to transcribe what was miraculously placed in their brains. A Bible verse solved any question, no matter how out of context the verse. No option existed for any tension in Scripture; the authors couldn't disagree with each other or have conflicting chronologies of events, because the singular voice of the divine couldn't contradict itself. Normal books had contradictions because they were written by normal people, but not the Bible. The Bible gave certainty, not confusion. I squeezed the ancient literary writing, with its poetic view of sequences and numbers, into my modern expectations for storytelling. I was a biblicist.

This phase didn't last forever. Luckily for me, the conflict that forced me into the next phase resided mostly in an intellectual sphere.

For others, the conflict happens experientially.

I told a version of the story about Bobby on the beach from chapter 3 in a podcast. I didn't call the story "Bobby on the Beach." I called it "Life's a Beach"—a title I changed after my wife told me the etymology of that phrase.

After I posted the somewhat vulgarly titled podcast, I received an email from a listener in Michigan named Norm.

> Been a podcast listener for about a year. Listened to L's a B yesterday.
>
> I was your guy. My tsunami came when my wife died in 2003. I lived in a world where you considered your situation, you leafed through the promises of God booklet until you found a verse that seemed to apply, then you said, "It's in the Bible; I believe it; that settles it." There are verses on prayer that have no conditions. During her illness, we quoted them with vigor.
>
> After her death, my faith slipped away steadily until I could see I was about to abandon faith in God entirely. It took until 2011 for me to begin to establish a new relationship with God.
>
> L's a B discussed the contracts we make with God. As you know, these contracts can be 100 percent based on scriptural words

and principles. The entire Old Testament resounds with words and examples that if we are faithful, God will be faithful and we will be protected and rewarded. As mentioned above, there are multiple prayer Scriptures without conditions, including the "Whatsoever ye ask in my name" verse.

To move forward after my tsunami, I have had to understand Scripture much differently.

Times of adversity cause growth or death. Either we grow into new levels, or our souls are choked by the cares of this world.

When the humanity of Scripture starts to be seen and expectations for the Bible aren't realized, the three options for what to do next become simple: bury our heads in the sand, ignoring the contradictions for as long as possible; jettison the now disappointing Bible; or shed our expectations and accept the Bible on its own terms.

Too Cold

The process isn't easy, because it's natural to transcend our previous levels of maturity and not retain the best of those previous levels. After my Michael Bay Bible stage, I was like Goldilocks after eating the porridge that was too hot. I swung the pendulum all the way to the other side, ending up with porridge that was too cold.

After earning a seminary degree, I was like a clumsy puppy with oversized paws and an uncontrollable wagging tail that knocked over coffee cups and toddlers. I was a sophomoric seminary grad with tools I didn't know how to use.

I reduced the Bible to an object I could master with my insights. I assumed there was one singular right reading and application for all biblical texts that could be deduced by proper scholarship.

And by proper scholarship, I meant my scholarship.

In my attempt to iron out the wrinkles, I dulled the two-edged sword's sharpness.

Whenever we act like a master, we remove the dignity and the humanity of whatever it is we've enslaved, whether that's a fellow human being or the Bible.

I stopped going to Scripture to find life, even though I diligently studied Scripture daily. And soon after, I stopped being able to sing.

Postanalytics

The scientific approach can help us get a better picture of God and Scripture, but there's always a part we can't master. Consider the influx of analytics in the world of professional sports.[2]

The world of modern sports has gone through a dramatic shift in analyzation that began with the baseball writer Bill James, who around 1980 first studied players' performances using statistical data. The new wave of data in all sports helped to make sense of the surprising value of often overlooked athletes like the basketball player Shane Battier.

Daryl Morey, Battier's former general manager with the Houston Rockets, described him as "a marginal NBA athlete." Battier didn't fill up a traditional stat sheet of points, rebounds, blocks, or assists. Over his thirteen years in the NBA, he averaged 8.6 points, 4.2 rebounds, and 1.8 assists per game. Yet his teams always performed substantially better when he was on the court.[3]

As Michael Lewis said, "Battier's game is a weird combination of obvious weaknesses and nearly invisible strengths. When he is on the court, his teammates get better, often a lot better, and his opponents get worse—often a lot worse."[4]

Until around 2010, many players in professional basketball were judged simply by basic statistics such as points, assists, and rebounds, none of which could explain why a player like Shane Battier could have mediocre basic stats but his team always seemed to do better when he was playing. And basic stats also couldn't explain the opposite: why some players could put up good stats, but their teams were perennial losers.

This is where analytics came in.

It removed the emphasis on traditional stats such as points and rebounds and instead focused on efficiency, because a basketball team is more than just the sum of its parts.

The popular modern analytic stat called plus-minus measures what happens to the score of a game when a player is on the court. Battier's career plus-minus is better than that of Hall of Fame players like Allen Iverson, Kevin McHale, Isaiah Thomas, and Dominique Wilkins, despite the fact that he averaged less than half of the points per game those Hall of Famers averaged.

Analytics has helped provide a much more precise understanding of just how much a player like Shane Battier helps a team win. The picture is clearer, but not perfect, because analysis can't offer a comprehensive understanding of how a basketball team functions. As two-time NBA MVP and current consultant for the Golden State Warriors Steve Nash once said, "We still haven't been able to put a number to the idea if guys like playing with each other."[5]

Advanced metrics provides a great deal of insight, but there's still an element of the game that cannot be reduced to a number.

In the same way, biblical scholarship can help us better understand biblical texts, and systematic theologies can help us better understand God, but an element remains that's irreducible to study.

When we think the sacred text is a book to be mastered instead of a book that masters us, our obsession with control will wall us off from the living water that we can find in the sacred text. When we think God can be systematized, we are in trouble, because the living God doesn't live in temples built by human hands or boxes of scholarship constructed by human minds.

The Bible becomes too hot without intellectual pursuit, and it becomes too cold when it's reduced to just an ancient text that can be deconstructed through academic analysis. An impotent and demythologized Bible often leads to a dried-up faith, and a lack of critical thinking leads people to continue to survive on milk when they should have moved on to solid food. Both extremes miss the complexity of what the Bible is trying to do to us.

Andrew Hawkins, a six-year NFL veteran, completed his master's in sports management at Columbia University while playing in the NFL. Hawkins said the following about the use of analytics in football: "Relying completely on analytics, that is just as bad as relying on no analytics. . . . My overall summary was that you have to have a balance."[6]

The same is true with the Bible. We shouldn't turn the Bible into a magic eight ball that we shake to make it tell us whatever we want, and we shouldn't make it a text that we can sterilize.

Complexity Is Its Validity

At times, I long for the simplicity created by my first view of the Bible. I miss the confidence that came from feeling I had God figured out. It's completely ridiculous to even write that sentence, but the naiveté was heartwarming in the moment.

I used to value the simplicity. Now I treasure the complexity.

The Bible's complexity isn't to be naively ignored or cynically deconstructed; instead, it's to be embraced as a source of its validity.

And to be perfectly clear, by the phrase "the Bible's complexity," I mean stuff that just doesn't make sense. For example, here's Matthew 27:9–10: "Then was fulfilled what had been spoken through the prophet Jeremiah, 'And they took the thirty pieces of silver, the price of the one on whom a price had been set, on whom some of the people of Israel had set a price, and they gave them for the potter's field, as the Lord commanded me.'"

It doesn't make sense that Matthew referenced the prophet Jeremiah when the quote wasn't from Jeremiah, but from Zechariah 11.

It also doesn't make sense that the account of David's census in 2 Samuel differs in a major way from the account in 1 Chronicles. See if you can catch it.

> Again the anger of the LORD was kindled against Israel, and he incited David against them, saying, "Go, count the people of Israel and Judah." (2 Sam. 24:1)

> Satan stood up against Israel, and incited David to count the people of Israel. (1 Chron. 21:1)

In 2 Samuel, God caused the census. In 1 Chronicles, it was Satan. That seems like a big difference.

Jesus's central talking point was the kingdom in Matthew, Mark, and Luke, but it was worded differently in each book. In Matthew's Gospel, which was written to a Jewish audience who wouldn't say the word *God*, Jesus used the phrase "kingdom of heaven." Heaven is the place where God exists, so "kingdom of heaven" was a roundabout way of saying "kingdom of God," which is the phrase Jesus used in Luke's Gospel. In John's Gospel, Jesus rarely talked about a kingdom but instead repeatedly mentioned eternal life. Jesus's most basic teachings don't even sound the same.

In a document trying to convince people to believe, some questionable material was included. In the Gospel accounts, the first spokespeople for the resurrection of Jesus were women. In the patriarchal culture of the first century, having women as the spokespeople would make no sense, because the testimony of women wasn't even considered valid.

In Matthew's Gospel, Matthew said this regarding followers of Jesus who had just seen the resurrected Jesus: "When they saw him, they worshiped him; but some doubted" (28:17). Some saw Jesus after he had been buried and then resurrected, and yet they still doubted. If they saw him and still didn't believe, what about people like us who've never seen him?

When I stopped trying to make the Bible fit my format, these contradictions transitioned from being disqualifiers to being authenticators. The human hand in the text shows that it wasn't a fabrication created by a single person in the dark recesses of some ivory tower but the honest testimony of a collection of people who'd experienced a life-altering event.

The humanity in the testimony, the lack of straight lines, fits with what modern research is teaching us about the unreliability of eyewitnesses. Witnesses' confidence in their correctness rises over time, and as their confidence rises, so does their credibility to jurors. But the actual ability of people to see and give a perfect account of events in comparison to a video recording is not even comparable. We might be confident in our memory, but rarely are we competent in our memories.[7]

If all the accounts in the Bible were smoothed out and every detail identical, that would raise red flags about the validity of the events, because it would seem as if the authors had conspired to tell the same fabricated story. The differences don't need to be evaded but celebrated, revealing the authentic testimony of a community's life-changing experience. The Bible's authority is in its complexity.

Biblicists, like I used to be, and many atheists read the Bible the same way with different conclusions. Both need the Bible to be perfect by modern standards to consider it inspired.

But the Bible, as it is, with all its complexities, is still sharp enough to divide soul from spirit, joints from marrow, and to judge the thoughts and intentions of the heart.

Unfailable

The Bible will not fail us because it points us to Jesus, and Jesus deserves our trust. The person of Jesus is without flaws, errors, or contradictions.

As Scripture tells us, Jesus is the true Word of God. Jesus is what is infallible. When the weight of validity is on Jesus, not an account of Jesus, we don't force the Bible to carry more weight than it should.

For our Muslim neighbors, the sacred miracle of their religion is the creation of the Koran. The prophet Muhammad had a role, a significant one, but what is paramount in Islam is the creation of the Koran. Muslims base their religion on their book.

Christianity's sacred miracle is not the Bible; it is Jesus. It is the Word becoming flesh. The words of the Bible testify about the sacred miracle, but the miracle of Christianity isn't Word becoming flesh and then regressing back into words.

The sacred miracle is the Word becoming flesh.

The Bible never claimed to be smooth—only sharp.

It's sharp, because it points to Jesus.

7

Bounding, Not Boxing

The wedding of Joel (Mr. "unable to answer five simple questions so I write a poetic story") and Katerina got me to the Dallas–Fort Worth airport waiting for a flight to New Orleans. I was soon joined in the terminal by a herd of white men wearing professional wrestling apparel. I quickly deduced that attending a class at Tulane's prestigious medical school wasn't the motivation for this herd's trip to the Big Easy.

Despite the headphones covering my ears, one loquacious man wearing a black shirt proclaiming the nonexistent biblical passage of Austin 3:16 asked about the location of my seats for Wrestlemania. Before I could explain that my agenda didn't include professional wrestling, he told me how excited he was to see his favorite wrestler, Stone Cold Steve Austin, the author of the aforementioned extrabiblical reference.

Despite the "do not disturb" sign that my noise-reducing headphones were intended to give, he sensed my ignorance of professional wrestling and launched into an unrequested tutorial. A few minutes into the diatribe, he sat stunned. Stone cold. His mouth abruptly closed, and his eyes widened, as did those of most of the men in the terminal. The entire herd's verbal abilities were put in a choke hold.

A figure the size of a Kenmore refrigerator, poorly hidden underneath a pair of dark glasses and a baseball hat, entered the gate. This figure, who could actually have been a shaved bear with great people skills, had more muscle mass than the rest of the people in the terminal combined.

The men in the terminal began moving like a pack of dogs circling a black bear.

An involuntary word fell out of the mouth of my slack-jawed friend. "Goldberg." As in Bill Goldberg, former NFL player turned pro wrestling champ, a name even I knew.

The motley crew waited to see who would make the first move. The first autograph seeker would surely face the wrath of this beast, but if they all attacked him at once, some could survive with their lives and an autograph. They knew strength existed in numbers, but they all stood still, either because no one wanted to be the sacrificial lamb or because they couldn't find their inhalers.

Like my beloved childhood dominoes, one fell into action, and then they all followed, swarming Goldberg for autographs and handshakes. Bill Goldberg, with a smile and a kind word, graciously received one ecstatic fan after another. Goldberg, the generous giant.

Upon returning from his chance to touch royalty and after waiting six minutes for his heart rate to drop below 140 beats per minute, my new friend continued with his tutorial on professional wrestling.

He explained the difference between smart fans, who understand what is happening, and ignorant fans, who "aren't in on the act." The ignorant fans who believe that professional wrestling is real are called marks.

As he explained that some adult human beings actually believe that professional wrestling isn't acting, my hope for the future of civilization went down for the count.

My friend made great effort to inform me that he wasn't a mark. He was a smark—short for smart marks, meaning they know that professional wrestling is fake, but they suspend their disbelief and act as though it is real. Doing so enables them to enjoy the show.

My new friend and I parted ways as we boarded the plane, but I couldn't stop thinking about what he had said. For the duration of my flight to New Orleans, I couldn't stop wondering if I too was a mark. Not for wrestling but for my religion. Had I suspended my disbelief of the divine so I could reap the benefits of something that wasn't real?

Had I knowingly looked past all the unbelievable aspects of faith so I could be numbed to the harsh realities of life?

Did the idea of God give me a reward that made me participate in the show?

Was I like a pro wrestling fan who had lost himself in a world of make-believe because he didn't want to be found in the real world?

That's where I was years ago in my "I can't sing" phase.

But it's not where I am anymore. This book was written from scars, not open wounds. The questions still exist, but they don't take me captive anymore, because I'm at peace with them. I can write about them with a degree of transparency, and I can do a set about my doubts at comedy clubs, because I've transcended the paralysis the doubts previously created, and now I can include the scars in my practice of faith.

The questions still exist, but they don't take away my voice anymore.

Greek Gods

My assistant, Jonathan, and I decided to do a sermon series together entitled "Christians Make the Best Atheists" as a play off the label early Christians received upon their baptism and renouncement of the other gods. At their baptism, early Christians faced west toward the epicenter of the gods, the Acropolis atop the city of Athens, and they spit at it and then renounced the devil and the gods. When they stopped worshiping gods such as Zeus, Athena, or Dionysus and began to worship only the Christian God, they were accused by others of being atheists.

Jonathan then twisted my arm into making a trip to Greece to record videos at the locations where these other gods were worshiped, including the Greek island of Delos for the god of the market, Hermes. But Delos is such a small island that there's no place to stay. And thus I'm staying for two nights on the Greek island of Mykonos, which is why I'm writing this paragraph overlooking the Aegean Sea.

The sacrifices I make for my job are almost unbelievable. But like the prophet Isaiah, I say, "Lord, here am I, send me." Especially when the destination is a Greek island.

Two days ago I sat in the top row of the two-thousand-year-old theater of Dionysus. Originally, it was just a hillside with a makeshift stage, but as the festival grew, seats were built into the hillside and a stone stage was laid. Morphing the religious festival that celebrated wine into a celebration of the arts, playwrights brought their stories to be performed. As I sat in the theater, a Brazilian actor drank a glass of wine and celebrated the history of her predecessors who had performed there while I pondered the similarities Dionysus had with Jesus, specifically resurrection.

Dionysus is believed to have brought forth the idea of the immortality of the soul, because he, like the vine, would die a painful death every year only to be brought back to life the next year.

In the Christian tradition, Jesus, the one who said, "I am the vine," died a painful death and was brought back to life and thus brought immortality of the soul to the world.

And that sounded a lot like Dionysus.

So which story is a myth and which is a historical event? Which one can we prove? Who is the mark in this situation, the Christian or the Greek?

This tensions sounds like a line from the atheist neuroscientist Sam Harris from a debate with megachurch pastor Rick Warren.

> Rick Warren: I say I accept that by faith. And I think it's intellectually dishonest for you to say you have proof that it didn't

happen. Here's the difference between you and me. I am open to the possibility that I am wrong in certain areas, and you are not.

Sam Harris: Oh, I am absolutely open to that.

Rick Warren: So you are open to the possibility that you might be wrong about Jesus?

Sam Harris: And Zeus. Absolutely.[1]

Like Warren, I'm open to the possibility that I am wrong. And like Harris, I know that I might also be wrong about the Greek gods.

Having doubts used to disturb me, but now I can accept their presence because Christian virtue calls us to honesty, including being honest about the limitations of our knowledge.

6.9 out of 7

Evolutionary biologist Richard Dawkins explained in a debate at Oxford University that he didn't want to be called an atheist, despite being described as the world's most famous atheist; instead, Dawkins preferred to be identified as an agnostic.

In his book *God Delusion*, Dawkins described a seven-point scale. A 1 on Dawkins's scale means "I know God exists." A 7 means "I know God doesn't exist." He claims to be a 6.9 because, as he says, "I think the probability of a supernatural creator existing is very, very low."[2] He's not willing to say he's a 7 because he doesn't fully know, and that's why he's not willing to call himself an atheist.

Even though I'd be on the opposite side of his scale at a 1.1, I agree with Dawkins's assessment that none of us can have complete certainty. When we expect to get rid of the leap by arriving at the end of the scale, the fact that we don't ever arrive there can create a resentment in our faith.

This is the flaw of many apologetics, Christian or atheist. They present a way to get all the way to 1 or 7 as if we will never wonder if our faith is akin to the belief of a pro wrestling fan or as if we will never wonder if we picked the wrong god to serve.

A friend who teaches Bible to American college students overseas in biblical locations says many students are disappointed after seeing the locations of key biblical events because they expected to have, upon arriving at the sacred sites, an aha moment that made their faith completely make sense and removed all doubt.

But it doesn't happen.

The expected epiphany moving them to 1 doesn't arrive, and so they end up like the crestfallen newly married husband expecting his spouse to cook him breakfast every morning. They are hungry for something they never get.

Always Been a Leap

Faith has always been a challenge, even for those who appear to have the easiest path to faith.

According to Scripture, the Jewish people were under the ruthless oppression of Pharaoh as slaves in Egypt. God chose Moses who, despite hearing this call from a talking bush that was on fire, and then seeing his staff turn into a snake and then back into a staff, and then seeing his healthy hand become leprous and then normal again, still doubted his abilities and did not have faith. Moses reluctantly went along with what God had asked of him only after God permitted him to bring his brother as his sidekick.

Then Moses and all the Israelites watched ten plagues happen to Egypt. The Nile River turned from water to blood. Frogs, gnats, and flies swarmed. Disease struck the Egyptian livestock, and boils inflicted the Egyptians. A hailstorm came, locusts invaded, and the sun went out. And then came the deeply problematic final plague of the death of Egypt's firstborn sons (which was couched as retribution for what Pharaoh had done to God's chosen, the Israelite people).

After all ten miraculous acts of God, the Israelites left Egypt only to be chased by Pharaoh and his army after Pharaoh changed his mind and decided he didn't want them to leave. When the Israelites appeared to be trapped between the army and the Red Sea, God parted the Red Sea, allowing Israel to walk through on dry land. Then members of Pharaoh's army, who had followed them into the dry path between the walls of water, were drowned by the water crashing down on them.

Israel was free after ten miracles plus the parting of the Red Sea spectacle. If anyone had reason to forever be a 1 on Dawkins's scale, it was these people, but almost immediately the Israelites displayed their lack of faith by complaining.

If the Bible is just a propaganda piece, as some critics argue, the Bible is not doing a good job. Why would the writers include the rampant unfaithfulness of God's chosen people despite excessive reason for them to be faithful?

The Bible isn't as much a propaganda piece as it is a library of books that testify to the community's faithful and unfaithful interactions with God.

Even for those near the miraculous ministry of Jesus, faith still wasn't easy. Followers of Jesus, even upon seeing the resurrected Jesus, still doubted.

The testimony of Scripture is that miracles have never sustained faith. Miracles give short-term boosts of fidelity, but they fail to create long-term obedience. Faith is a leap, and it will continue to be a leap until faith becomes sight.

What matters most isn't the absence of questions but the presence of faith-sustaining practices.

Orthopraxy

And now, a Jimmy Fallon joke: "Thank you, people who only go to church on Easter Sunday, for being the religious equivalent of flossing ten minutes before your dentist appointment."[3]

If you show up for a dental appointment having flossed only one time in six months, and that one time was that morning, you will have bloody gums but not clean teeth. To get the benefit of flossing—just like with spiritual disciplines, including going to church—you must practice repeatedly.

Faith isn't just about what we think; it's also about what we do. Christians have spent so much time focusing on right thinking (orthodoxy) that we've forgotten to focus on right living (orthopraxy), which has always been at the heart of the way of Jesus. Deep faith doesn't come from what we think but from what we do repeatedly.

In John's Gospel, believing is always a verb, never a noun. Belief isn't something we possess but an activity in which we participate. Faith isn't something we have as much as it is something we do.[4]

Our modern emphasis on religion being about thinking over living wouldn't have made sense in the first century, since that's not how they used the word *religion*. Church historian Larry Hurtado says of the Greek word used to describe religion, "In Paul's own time, however, the Greek word *ioudaïsmos* seems to have designated more the activity of promoting a Jewish way of life exhibited particularly in the observance of the commandments of Jewish law."[5]

Since Paul's time and before, the Jewish or Christian religion wasn't just about the ideas we think but the life that we live. Yet that's how we use the word *believe* now.

Usually, we say "believe" when we aren't completely sure about something. For example, "I'm not sure, but I believe there's a Chipotle two miles down the road."

But belief doesn't just cover intellectual gaps. Belief is that thing in which we invest our lives, as in, "I believe that Chipotle is the future of fast-service restaurants, so I'm going to get a second mortgage on my house and invest that money into opening a Chipotle franchise in my neighborhood."

The first example is about an idea that we can't presently confirm. The second example is about a conviction that reroutes our existence.

Belief isn't just about the space created by intellectual inconsistencies; it's about the direction of our lives. To believe in something is to let that something become our source of direction and of understanding our existence. We can believe every piece of information about the Bible, but the information is just trivia if it doesn't shape how we live. God makes space for those who doubt ideas and knowledge because faith isn't about what we think of trivia. Faith is about whom we trust.

The benefits of faith come from the practices we do repeatedly. So even when our ideas about God are in flux and we question the legitimacy of Christianity, our faith doesn't have to be in flux if we continue to remember our disciplines.

Training

In the fall of my first year on the track team at Abilene Christian University, I was in the sparsely occupied weight room on a Friday afternoon. An upperclassman with a couple national championships in track's hardest race, the 400-meter hurdles, walked over to me in the corner of the weight room. He put an arm on my shoulder and turned me toward the center of the weight room so I could see all the vacant machines and empty stations.

"Luke, do you see that?"

"Um . . . no," I said, since I saw an almost empty weight room.

"That's the difference between being an All-American and being a national champion: Friday afternoons."

Not doing the work on Fridays in the off-season when everyone wants to be out having fun prevents good athletes from becoming national champions. A successful athlete knows that success comes from continually putting in the work, even when you don't feel like it.

Like an athlete who must continue to run in season and out of season to win, if we want to have faith, we have to remember our disciplines even when we don't want to. Even when we have intellectual issues with God, even when the Bible doesn't make sense to us, even when God doesn't live up to our expectations, we have to continue to practice disciplines that keep our faith afloat.

In the story of Jonah, a prophet of God ran away from the Creator of the universe by getting on a boat. Surprisingly, God can't be outrun. Who would have guessed that the Creator of the universe doesn't lose at the game of hide-and-seek?

A storm showed up threatening the boat's buoyancy, so what did the others on the boat with Jonah do? They threw cargo deemed nonessential overboard.

Too often, when our faith is in crisis, we throw overboard the practices that actually have the ability to keep us afloat.

We stop showing up to do the work.

We give up on prayer.

We give up on confession.

We give up on the sacraments.

We give up on community.

Research has shown that when we think about God, our brains change, new connections are made, and neural activity begins in different parts of the brain. But when our faith becomes dormant, that part of our brains grows dormant.

Similar to the way an athlete's muscles weaken when they stop training, our faith atrophies when we stop practicing it. When our faith is formed through daily Scripture reading and then we toss overboard the practice, our faith atrophies. Which is why what often weakens our faith the most during a faith crisis isn't the questions, the doubts, or the lack of certainty but the absence of faith-sustaining practices. If we want to continue to see the beauty in our faith, we have to show up even when we don't want to.

If you tell me what you do repeatedly, I can tell you what you are going to become.

Our world is already at capacity for people who can tell us what's wrong with the faith of others, because it's easier to tear down than it is to build. Tearing down can be done in a day, but constructing a sustaining faith requires a lifetime of practice.

Into the Crowd

I've heard a rumor that Bono, U2's lead singer, on nights when he doesn't have the voice to hit the high notes, will still play the songs with the high notes, but when it's time to hit them, he will leave center stage, go out in the crowd, turn the mic to the audience, and let them sing.

When he can't hit the notes, he lets the crowd sing for him.

When you have no voice to sing, follow Bono's lead. Head into the great cloud of witnesses and let them sing for you.

The Bible contains a story about a paralyzed man whose friends wanted to bring him to Jesus, but the house that Jesus was in was overcrowded, and there was no way for them to get through the door. So they climbed up on the roof, removed the roof tiles, and lowered the man down on his mat in front of Jesus.

Jesus eventually healed the paralyzed man, but before he healed him, Jesus observed the faith of the man and his friends. Luke's account says, "When [Jesus] saw their faith" (5:20).

Their faith.

Whose faith did Jesus see that caused the healing?

Their faith. Not his faith. When the man's faith wasn't enough, his friends' faith carried him.

One of the practices central to sustaining faith during crisis is leaning into community, because a faith journey on one's own rarely goes far. As Proverbs says, "A brother is born for adversity" (17:17 KJV). When our faith is struggling, we need brothers and sisters who can sustain us.

As a college student, I heard a preacher say that if there were two men, one with a great marriage but no close male friends and one with a bad marriage but close, godly friends, he would wager that the person most likely not to have an affair would be the man with the bad marriage but close, godly friends. He was spot on about the value of community.

Often, we emphasize the "go off in the woods alone" spiritual disciplines. The "just you and God" practices, like reading the Bible and praying, are valuable, but if I had to prescribe only one practice for someone in a faith crisis, it would be to engage in a consistent, intentional gathering of believers where honesty and transparency are valued. We are only as sick as our secrets, and if the secret of our struggles is never shared, our souls get sicker.

We need the people who can sing our song when we don't have a voice. We need the people who will lower us down through the roof when we can't stand. And the first way to find that community is by being that type of friend for someone else.

Santa and God

In Greek mythology, Thetis dipped her son Achilles in the river Styx, making him invincible, except for the part of his body by which she held him when he was submerged, the heel. Why Thetis didn't just dip Achilles a second time while holding him elsewhere is a separate conversation. Years later the great warrior Achilles died because of an arrow that struck him in his unbaptized spot, his heel.

When my eight-year-old daughter asked, "Is God like Santa?" it was as if an arrow went into the Achilles' heel of my soul. I'd always hated that we lie to our kids about Santa's existence. When we say that Santa comes down the chimney or that the Tooth Fairy places money under their pillow or that the Easter Bunny brings candy, we establish a precedent of basing large, meaningful chunks of life on unseen things that will later be revealed as fiction. This creates a foundation for the critical thinkers to one day say, "I don't believe in God, because God is just another lie that we were told to promote good behavior, like Santa."

I didn't have a better solution for what to do with the festivities of Christmas, so I went along with the lie. Such is the banality of evil.

When Avery asked, "Is God like Santa?" I was faced with a decision either to continue the Christmas lie so my family could enjoy the holidays together or to tell her the truth for her faith's best interest.

The appropriate response would have been, "Your mother and I can tell you about this together after she returns home from Target." But as I told Lindsay multiple times over the following months, I had to make a split-second decision. I didn't have time to think through every possible scenario, much like when Captain Sully landed the plane on the Hudson River after the engines failed.

So I heroically told my daughter the truth.

(Lindsay and I had a minor disagreement over which captain from a Tom Hanks movie I was in that moment. I thought I was Captain Sully. She thought I was the person who claimed "I am the captain now" in *Captain Phillips* because I had pirated the joy of Christmas from her.)

When Lindsay returned home, I told her I had told Avery that Santa isn't real. She immediately began to cry, and she continued to cry even after she left the living room to go through our bedroom into our bathroom. I know she continued to cry because I could hear her sobbing over the sound of the shower. To be fair to me, we don't have great water pressure, so our shower isn't super loud.

Everyone who has heard this story thinks I ruined Christmas for my family—except for one brave preacher friend who told me that he would never say it publicly and that he would take his opinion with him to the grave, but he thinks I did the right thing.

Despite everyone thinking I'm the Grinch, I don't care. Because guess what? The Grinch isn't real either.

Now that Lindsay is talking to me again, I understand my wife's heartbreak. She was grieving the last year of our oldest daughter's childlike wonder for Christmas. My wife invests a great deal in making Christmas a day that brings great joy to our family, and she knew that once Avery knew about Santa, the day would never be the same again. Parenting mixes joy and grief, because every moment that you have with your child is also one less that you will have with them before they leave. This was a major milestone that she unexpectedly had to grieve.

I was grieving the struggle of faith that I don't want my daughters to have. I don't want faith to be any more difficult than it needs to be because of problematic holiday storytelling, unhealthy views of Scripture, or the dragging of biblical texts into issues they aren't addressing. The "letting go" of faith doesn't mean we have to stop loving the Lord with all our mind. There's a reason to learn from the ways people throughout history and people today have tried to make sense of faith. And there's a reason to make faith as reasonable as possible.

Letting go doesn't mean we must digress into anti-intellectualism or water down the meaning of the word *truth*. Just because we want something to be true doesn't mean it is. But letting go does mean we must admit our limitations and our inability to master what Truth is.

When Jesus said to believe, he was not providing a list of ideas to check off. He was offering an invitation to a way of life that is shaped around practices that force us into the cruciform posture of vulnerability, despite the way that cynicism, discouragement, and resistance attempt to curve us in upon ourselves. Belief is a commitment to a lifestyle of disciplines and practices that keep us leaping even when we don't want to leap.

Blessed Are Those Who Leap

When the resurrected Jesus appeared to the disciples, the one who probably needed to see him the most, the patron saint of skeptics, "doubting Thomas,"[6] was absent. Thomas would later declare that unless he saw the nail marks with his own eyes and touched them with his own hands, he wouldn't believe—an understandable sentiment for many of us proof seekers.

A week later the disciples were gathered in a home behind a locked door, and the resurrected Jesus somehow appeared and stood among them.

> Then [Jesus] said to Thomas, "Put your finger here; see my hands. Reach out your hand and put it into my side. Stop doubting and believe." . . . Then Jesus told him, "Because you have seen me, you have believed; blessed are those who have not seen and yet have believed." (John 20:27, 29 NIV)

When we believe without seeing the proof that we think will permanently remove doubt, there is a blessing. Many of us assume the blessing will arrive when we can see with our eyes and touch with our hands all the proof we desire, but Jesus says it's the opposite. We are blessed when what we expect to see isn't there but we still believe. We are blessed when the knowledge we possess doesn't pass our desired threshold of information and yet we still trust. We are blessed when we let go of our expectations for what God is supposed to be so we can receive what God is.

There is a blessing for those who believe without seeing, because in the leap of faith, there is beauty.

Beauty of the Leap

I've always thought that one of the most impressive athletic feats is the high jump. It's simple yet stunning. A person takes a handful of steps and then flings their entire body over a bar that is often a foot over their head. Truly awe inspiring.

We don't have to understand anything about the sport to marvel at the feat of jumping seven feet in the air. When we leap, we fight ourselves free from gravity's force for just a split second. We momentarily let go of the force that keeps us grounded.

Faith has always been about letting go. Jesus said that if we want to follow him, we must deny ourselves.

We must let go of our control.

We must let go of our expectations.

We must let go of our lives.

As Richard Rohr said, "All great spirituality is about letting go."[7]

Humanity is about holding on. Spirituality is about letting go.

St. Augustine described the effects of sin in Latin as *incurvatus in se*, which means "curved inward on oneself."[8] Sin, the cosmic resistance to God's intention for God's creation, turns us inward to focus only on our own wants, desires, and needs. Like chronic arthritis can squeeze infected hands into a perpetual fist, sin can contort us into a closed-off posture toward the world.

Sin shrivels us up.

Jesus opens us up.

The clearest picture of what God is like is Jesus hanging on a cross. The Romans stretched his arms wide and nailed his hands to the old rugged cross, where he hung naked, completely vulnerable to the worst the world has to offer.

Sin is the arthritic hand clenched shut.

The way of Jesus is arms spread wide, vulnerable, and open toward all.

Blessed are those who believe without seeing, because they learn to place their souls in the open and vulnerable posture of Jesus.

At track practice my sophomore year in college, I warmed up every day with the same pole. Pole vaulters typically have multiple poles with varying lengths and test weights. This was the shortest and easiest pole for me to use no matter how slow I felt or how windy it was.

As my coach often told me, "Luke, you are so slow that grass keeps growing under your feet." This pole was the safety blanket that someone with my speed needed.

For my first warm-up jump of the day, I went to my spot, twenty steps from the mat, with the pole in my hands, my right hand at a ninety-degree angle across my chest and my left hand down by my left hip, and both feet together.

I put my left foot back, rocked my weight back onto my left foot, and popped my right toe off the ground. Then I pressed down on my right heel, shot my left leg forward, and sprinted twenty steps. On step twenty, I planted my pole in the metal box at the base of the landing mat and leapt off my right foot, kicking my feet above my head.

As I was upside down directly over the metal box, I heard a loud crack like the sound of a rifle. Almost instantaneously, the support from the pole vanished and I felt a smack across my back. My feet stopped going up and instead began flipping backward over my head. I was completely out of control, upside down, disoriented.

A split second later I landed on the front edge of the mat, my head just six inches away from the metal box, with a four-foot piece of my trusted pole in my hands and the other pieces scattered around the mat.

The pole had snapped, and so had my confidence.

Minutes later I went back to the end of the runway with a new pole. I stood there trying to coerce myself to jump. My left foot would step back, my right toes would pop up, but I couldn't make myself go forward. Like a broken record repeating the same two seconds of a song, I kept rocking back and forth without ever moving forward.

I couldn't make myself leap, because leaping would make me susceptible to the serious injury I had almost experienced, and my brain wouldn't let me put my body back into that precarious position.

Leaping makes us vulnerable. Maybe the reason faith is supposed to be a leap is because that's the only way we follow Jesus into a vulnerable posture toward the world.

Certainty clenches around conclusions, making fists to punch.

Leaping contorts us into the vulnerable posture of Jesus, enabling us to love and embrace the world.

Benefits of the Doubt

In a story told twice in Matthew's Gospel,[9] the religious leaders asked Jesus to confirm his identity by performing a miracle, but Jesus didn't play their game. He replied, "A wicked and adulterous generation asks for a sign! But none will be given it except the sign of the prophet Jonah" (12:39 NIV). Jesus then left them and went away.

Our obsession with eradicating all skepticism with certainty by providing explicit signs isn't shared by Jesus. I bet Jesus was aware of the short-term effect that the miraculous has on faith—the temporary boost in mental confidence—but what Jesus wants is more than just a transient boost in confidence. Jesus wants us to experience the blessing of leaping.

Peter said, "Always be ready to make your defense to anyone who demands from you an accounting for the hope that is in you" (1 Pet. 3:15). Maybe we should stop reading this as a command to weaponize intellectual arguments with clenched fists and instead see it as a call to be able to articulate the blessing we've experienced through a lifestyle of practices that have shaped us into Jesus's cruciform posture, because that's an answer that deserves to be heard.

Pastor Practices

Now a word about pastors with doubts.

When I was in college, I waited tables at one of my then-favorite restaurants, which served amazingly soft rolls with cinnamon butter and allowed you to throw peanut shells on the floor, a brilliant combination of two of my favorite things: carbs and littering.

But after working there, I never want to eat there again. I will find my carbs and littering opportunities elsewhere.

For those of you who've worked at a restaurant, I bet you can sympathize, although this phenomenon isn't confined to the restaurant business.

I have a friend in the music industry who, when he's driving, will only listen to talk radio because he doesn't want to hear work. I have a friend in sports radio who would rather not talk sports when we have lunch, because talking sports is work. When my uncle, a cat veterinarian, sees a stray cat, he doesn't see it as a lost pet but as spare parts.

Okay. That one might not be true.

Our occupations alter the way we experience the subject matter they entail. Because my job is faith, my job alters the way I experience faith because faith can be reduced to just a commodity in which I trade. I've been rewarded for having a faith that appears strong since I started preaching as an eighteen-year-old. As T. S. Eliot said, "The last temptation is the greatest treason: To do the right deed for the wrong reason."[10] That treason is an ever present temptation for people who do right things for a career.

I've also had the amazing privilege of making my life's work something I care deeply about. I've had to learn how to name the ways in which resistance can take my critical thinking and use it to curve my soul in on itself. Everyone's journey includes challenges; this just happens to be mine.

This also explains why I have the worst dog in the world. My wife and our daughters wanted a dog. I love dogs, but I didn't want a dog at this point in our lives. We had previously had three beloved dogs that had already gone up to the big dog park in the sky. I didn't think we had the time or the energy for another dog. All the girls in my family thought differently. It was one versus four, and I was not doing a good job of holding off the attackers.

In the middle of my own battle of Thermopylae, I took a trip to Tennessee for my first interview with N. T. Wright. After the interview, we headed to downtown Nashville to get some lunch. While I was waiting to go into a pizza place, Lindsay called. My assistant, Jonathan, was already outside the car, and I waved for him to wait a minute as I immediately sensed concern in her voice.

When she said, "Adalyn just went to the doctor, and I've got some bad news," my stomach dropped.

An itchy arm, a rash across her stomach, and a headache had taken our middle daughter to the doctor. The doctor, who knows Lindsay both as a parent and as a nurse who works with her in the hospital, informed Lindsay that those symptoms, along with Adalyn's month-long low-grade fever, necessitated some blood tests, including one for leukemia.

When Lindsay said that Adalyn was being tested for leukemia, I broke down. And my first thought was that if my daughter had leukemia, she should at least get a dog, the typical "Dad has to do something to fix this" response. I don't think dogs cure leukemia, but getting one made sense in the moment. So I told Lindsay to tell the girls that we were getting a dog when I got home.

My daughter didn't have leukemia, and the only reason I knew it was a possibility was because my wife is a nurse. The doctor knew that Lindsay would know what the ambiguous phrase "some blood tests" would mean with those symptoms, so she was straightforward. She never would have said "test for leukemia" if an uneducated person like me had been there; she would have just said "some tests."

The curse of being in the medical field is you know what's behind every ambiguous phrase, and you know the worst-case scenarios.

When your profession is spirituality, you've (theoretically) studied the complexities and have some awareness of the debates and discussions. So you carry an extra weight.

(How pastors can act as if there is no complexity to issues that have divided thoughtful Christians for centuries and instead just pompously preach their opinion as the only option an honest and intelligent person could take is another story for another time.)

Every path has particular obstacles and therefore requires particular practices. As someone who talks about faith for a living, I've had to develop the practice of not talking about part of my faith.

I was running with a new set of wireless headphones when a warning beep began going off informing me that the headphones' battery was low. I was faced with a very First World problem: What am I going to do when the music fades? Am I going to keep running even when there's no music to entertain me? Can I keep up this pace when the only sounds I hear are my own breathing and my feet on concrete?

My charismatic friends would say that what happened next was God speaking to me.

A question popped into my head: What's going to happen to your faith when the music fades?

What are you going to do with your faith when you don't have an audience to speak to? What will happen to your faith when you don't have the external motivators causing you to believe?

My audit of my faith revealed that I wasn't keeping enough of my faith for me. Too much of my own journey was being used for my job.

When entering into silence or opening up the sacred text is always done in a professional setting, little is left for one's own soul. I had to create a practice of saving some spiritual experiences solely for my own formation. I didn't have to share everything, because some moments are to be cherished on their own.[11]

In the same way, I don't want every experience I have with my kids to become a social media post, because then every moment devolves into a potential photo shoot. The moment itself doesn't matter as much. The moments need to live on their own. They don't need to be shared online or spoken of in a sermon.

A Jewish tradition involves not writing the full name of the divine. Instead, the shorthand "G-d" is used because some things shouldn't be spoken.

For all of us, some things just don't need to be spelled out for everyone else. We can share them with our closest people, not with the crowd. Especially for those of us who talk about God in public, we need to make sure that we also talk to God in private and keep those conversations there. Certain experiences with God can't be explained. When we are constantly putting those experiences into words, those experiences lose their vitality. There are times when Word becomes flesh; we need to let it stay as flesh and not give in to the temptation to let it revert back into words.

Secrecy is a practice that people like me often need to partake in to keep our souls from curving inward because, as Thomas Merton said, "If we have no silence, God is not heard in our music."[12]

Talking about Practice

Not every person connects with every practice to the same degree. Our stage of life, our experiences, and our personality shape which practices are most formative for us. For example, the desert fathers prescribed fasting to those struggling with sexual sin, because learning to discipline the body's natural longing for food could be transferred to the body's natural longing for sex. For those struggling with greed, the prescribed discipline might be a pilgrimage to a developing country to serve and live among those with much less. For the prideful, it might be extra confession of sin and failure. Different terrain determines the value of different practices. No matter the terrain of our path, the one constant is the need for some practices that sustain our faith.

For many of us, we've tried to leave our doubts, but our doubts have never left us. But as long as we don't let go of the practices that continually put us into the posture of Jesus, the presence of doubts doesn't necessitate the absence of belief.

8

God over god

Baggage Free

In Athens there's a statue of Aphrodite, the goddess of love, leaning against a smaller statue of Aphrodite. It's a fitting metaphor for how we feel about love. We love love.

When we initially fall in love, we are usually in love with the concept of love, not the actual person in front of us. The intoxicating power of love blinds us from seeing the person's actual humanity, and so we fall in love with a blurry concoction of expectations that we confuse for our beloved.

Now let's play a game. It's called "Who is the most unromantic, the psychiatrist or the theologian?"

First the psychiatrist, Scott Peck:

> Falling in love is not real love. . . . [They] realize that they are
> not one with their beloved. . . . At this point they can either dis-
> solve the relationship or they can begin working towards love.[1]

Put that to a beat and you've got yourself a chart-topping pop song.

Now the theologian, Stanley Hauerwas:

> The assumption is that there is someone just right for us. It
> fails to appreciate the fact that we always marry the wrong
> person. . . . The primary problem is learning how to love and
> care for the stranger to whom you find yourself married.[2]

Neither of these two will end up writing Hallmark cards, but they do accurately pinpoint the distortion of love in America. When we fall in love, we rarely fall in love with the actual person; we fall in love with the idea of love.

As the relationship matures, we are given the opportunity to get to know the actual person, with their flaws, their short-comings, and even some of their previously unseen strengths. Only when we can name their dust and their divinity can we actually love them.

Adolescent love looks for someone without baggage. Mature love discards the naive assumption that any person is baggage free and instead looks for ways to lighten the load of the loved one.

This journey from naive idealism to mature acceptance is the natural progression of any relationship, even a relationship with the divine.

god to God

The move to maturity in faith involves accepting the revealed God instead of an ideal god.

If the leap of faith we are taking is toward Christianity, our view of God is built on the revelation of God in the flesh as the person of Jesus of Nazareth. According to Scripture, in this Jewish man, the fullness of God was revealed. As Jesus said, "Anyone who has seen me has seen the Father" (John 14:9 NIV). The revealed God is Jesus; the ideal god is the accumulation of our expectations. If our description of the Christian God doesn't look like Jesus of Nazareth, then we are looking at our ideal, not the real.

If we say that God is too holy to be around sinners, then that's our expectations, because the revealed God spent so much time with the most shamed sinners of the first century, including drunks, that some people assumed Jesus of Nazareth was a drunk.

If we think that God doesn't enter into suffering and pain, then that's our expectations, because Jesus of Nazareth experienced the worst humanity has to offer.

If our god doesn't fit on a cross, then we have created a deity based on our expectations.

Differentiating between the ideal and the real doesn't come easily. Jesus's own disciples spent a substantial amount of time with him and still couldn't differentiate. After Jesus finished a teaching about the Son of Man having to suffer, be rejected, and be killed, Peter pulled Jesus aside to give him some notes—as if he and Jesus were two baby preachers learning how to preach—because the idea of Jesus suffering didn't fit Peter's expectations. Jesus responded by saying to Peter, "Get behind me, Satan!" (Matt. 16:23).

It's bad to have a friend call you Satan.

It's really bad when that friend is God.

But after Peter's expectations were deconstructed, the faith that was resurrected in Peter turned out to be a faith upon which Jesus could build the church. Initially, Peter followed the suffering-free god of his expectations; eventually, he followed the crucified God.

The eighteenth-century French philosopher Voltaire said, "In the beginning God created man in His own image, and man has been trying to repay the favor ever since." We choose the ideal over the revealed because the revealed does to us what Jesus did to Peter: it offends.

God in the abstract is acceptable.

God incarnate is problematic.

Baby Preachers

When you are a baby preacher, everyone loves you. Or at least they love the idea of a baby preacher. The institution of the church has given so many people identity, community, and direction in life. Without baby preachers replenishing the church's pulpits, the continuation of this foundational institution would be in jeopardy, which is why church people usually have an appreciation for new volunteers to captain the ship.

When you are a baby preacher, no one knows how you will want to steer the ship. All church people know is that they need people like you to assume the helm to ensure their church continues. Thus, baby preachers are a blank canvas on which people project their hopes.

Eventually, the real emerges, and the preacher's convictions are no longer under the surface. For some passengers, this course is a godsend; for others, it seems like a titanic mistake.

The idea of a god who embodies our expectations is easier to stomach than a specific God, because we are more comfortable with who we want God to be. All our hopes and dreams of what the divine should do are still on the table. When God is revealed, in a specific person with a specific message, we might not like where the ship is heading. But in this realization that God isn't our god, we are offered the invitation to maturity. We can relinquish our claims over God and instead let God make claims over us. In this unnerving process of letting go of our naive ownership of God, we are able to receive who God actually is.

Believe but Don't Like

One sign that we are maturing is when we find ourselves believing in a God we don't always like. Maturity in faith has always required acceptance of how God doesn't fit into the mold of what we would like God to be.

Jesus had just finished an offensive teaching that caused many to stop following him. Jesus then turned to the twelve disciples and asked if they too wanted to leave. Peter responded, "Lord, to whom can we go? You have the words of eternal life" (John 6:68).

The God we might like would be heavy on the divine but light on the dust.

The God we might like would eradicate all suffering.

The God we might like would provide indisputable miracles.

The God we might like wouldn't ask us to do unthinkable things such as forgive or show generosity.

The God we might like would go to a cross for us but wouldn't ask us to carry our own cross.

But like Peter, we stay, even when none of our expectations are fulfilled, because in God we've found life.

Why do we worship God when God doesn't always fit our definition of good? Because unlike the transience we're surrounded by, the transcendent offers something eternal. It doesn't provide the protection of an exoskeleton, but it becomes the endoskeleton around which we can build our existence.

When we discover that our spouse doesn't match our ideal, we stay because we've found love.

When we discover that God isn't our ideal, we continue in faith because we've experienced something transcendent. We've experienced everlasting life, and where else can we go?

Lose Your Britches, Save Your Breath

How about a wave story?

Yes, another wave story.

On a cool evening, you're walking along the shore, just a step away from the water's edge, making sure your boots stay dry. The chilly ocean breeze, partially blocked by your denim jacket, isn't completely unbearable. You momentarily wish for the heat of summer, but not for long, because you can always add layers in the winter; in the summer, however, you can only disrobe so much without getting arrested.

You are lost in the winter versus summer debate, oblivious to the growing swell over your shoulder. The aptly named sneaker wave gets closer as you wonder which quotation to attach to the obligatory sunset picture you are about to post on Instagram.

Just as you settle on a lyric from a late '90s rock band, you are flattened by a wave. Your phone flies out of your hands, your face slams into the sand, and the wave spins you up the shore. Seconds later the undertow pulls you into the sea.

The spin cycle has left you confused and disoriented. The light seems to be coming from below your feet, so you try to swim toward the light to get to the surface.

Something immediately becomes apparent—it's much harder to swim when you're fully dressed. Your leather boots, now fully saturated, feel like concrete, and the saltwater has turned your denim jacket into a straitjacket. You can't fight both the undertow and your attire. Your singular concern now is staying alive, not keeping your wardrobe. You kick off your boots and shed your jacket. As your attire becomes a peace offering to placate the angry water, you paddle to the surface.

The boots and the jacket were great at keeping you warm on the shore, but they are a detriment to your survival in the water.

As a kid learning how to swim at the YMCA, I was told that the first thing you do if you accidentally fall in the water while dressed is take your jeans off, because the embarrassment of being seen in your underwear is not as bad as not being seen while you sink. On dry land, it's great to have pants on. Chances are if you ever see me, I will be wearing them. But if you are trying to stay afloat, you are going to have to shed some layers.

In emergencies, the brain does the same move toward simplicity by shedding secondary responsibilities. The fight-or-flight response reduces blood flow to certain areas of the brain, causing the brain to become almost a lizard brain, which has the singular focus of staying alive. This is why, during combat, fine motor skills such as turning off a gun's safety switch or loading bullets into a clip can become extremely difficult for the inexperienced. The brain sheds secondary responsibilities, such as manual dexterity, to focus on the most essential of tasks, such as breathing.

In a crisis of faith, we need to take the same approach. When faced with losing our expectations or losing our faith, we need to be able to shed secondary beliefs.

Scripture set the precedent for not seeing every practice or belief as having the same level of importance. Jesus prioritized loving God and loving people as the greatest commandments. Paul put forth the belief that is of first importance: "For I handed on to you as of *first importance* what I in turn had received: that Christ died for our sins in accordance with the scriptures, and that he was buried, and that he was raised on the third day in accordance with the scriptures" (1 Cor. 15:3–4, emphasis added).

Far too many people lose their faith because they see faith as an all-or-nothing proposition. If one part of their faith falls, then all of it collapses. But faith often goes through its own death, burial, and resurrection. Certain layers must be discarded so that a new, more mature faith can be resurrected.

At the core of Christianity is death, burial, and resurrection, so should we really be surprised that we experience death, burial, and resurrection in our spirituality?

This death, burial, and resurrection isn't an event but a lifestyle.

Trust the Process

I hope this book helps people find their faith after they've experienced a disappointment, and for that reason, I've included my own story of faith after disappointment.

When asked about being two-faced in a debate with Stephen Douglas, Abraham Lincoln is said to have replied, "If I had another face, do you think I'd wear this one?" If I had another story to tell other than my own, I would tell it, because I don't want to give the impression that my story has been completed. But alas, this is the only story I have.

I don't make any assumption that my faith has arrived at its destination. What I have arrived at is the conviction that faith is not a destination but a process. If faith isn't moving forward, it's dying.

Paul said that we forget what's behind and press on to what's ahead[3] because faith isn't meant to be static or still. Faith is a continual pressing forward. The invitation to enter into the way of Jesus is constant.

When I was a grad student, an undergrad student from the Baptist school in town asked me to disciple him. As a twenty-one-year-old myself, I didn't know what discipling was supposed to look like, but despite my reservations, I met with him.

I decided that at our first mentoring session I was going to talk to him about humility. Before I could even get to minute two of my talk on humility, the college student interrupted me to say, "Yes, Luke, I learned humility a year ago." And then he proceeded to tell me all he knew about humility.

There is something intuitively wrong about interrupting someone as they describe humility to tell them what you know about humility.

When we say that we've arrived at humility, um . . . no, we haven't.

When we think that our faith has arrived, um . . . no, it hasn't.

Paul, the author of the most books in the Bible, didn't even think he had arrived. He said, "Not that I have already obtained this or have already reached the goal; but I press on to make it my own" (Phil. 3:12).

No one's faith ever fully arrives.

Maya Angelou once said, "I'm always amazed when people walk up to me and say, 'I'm a Christian.' I think, 'Already? You already got it?' I'm working at it, which means that I try to be as kind and fair and generous and respectful and courteous to every human being."[4]

To choose faith is to choose to continually work on moving to the rhythm of death, burial, and resurrection and to acknowledge that though outwardly we might be wasting away, inwardly we are being renewed day by day. To choose faith is to be part of a process of transformation from one degree of likeness to another while shedding what we have outgrown.

Getting Change

Faith is not about finding the right point but about finding the right process. But a commitment to one point is easier than a commitment to a process, because change is hard.

We can see this in the way churches struggle over worship styles. Debating "worship style" sounds much more sophisticated than the more accurate description, which is debating who gets to control the radio station.

People love their preferences and usually wait until their generation gets power so they can finally get their way. And then as their generation ages, they exhibit the same selfish obsession with keeping their preferences as did the previous generation, whom they swore they would never be like. We all do become our parents at some point.

Most of us commit to a specific change instead of a process of change. The reason advertisers pay top dollar to attract the coveted eighteen-to-twenty-five-year-old age demographic is because during those years most people make the choices that they maintain for their entire lives.

Change is hard, but spiritual maturity involves learning to embrace the process of letting go with the peaceful disposition of Jesus.

I did a funeral for a small-town judge who spent his life serving his community and loving his family. He was a quiet man who never raised his voice at home or even his gavel in his courtroom. For decades, he would come home from the courtroom for lunch. After eating, he would take a ten-minute nap on the living room floor with his feet crossed. Every day his family would find him lying on the floor, head on a pillow, and one foot on top of the other.

When they found him asleep for the last time after his eighth decade, they found him in his bed, just as they had found him every day on the floor, with one foot crossed over the other.

Maybe he positioned his feet this way because of the muscle memory ingrained over decades. Maybe this was just a natural posture for him after doing it for so many years.

Or maybe the peaceful posture of his feet reflected the peacefulness of his soul as he was about to enter into the great unknown because of his trust in God—a trust that had been developed by decades of faithfulness to God.

All spirituality is about the hard process of letting go and denying ourselves. Spirituality is not about letting go once but about repeatedly shedding control until we arrive on our deathbed and finally let go for good.

The hope is that by the time we reach our deathbed, we've learned, through the way God has sustained us in each time of letting go throughout our lives, to have faith in God. When we let go for good, we've already built up the trust and the muscle memory of loosening our grip that come from having a lifetime of reliance on God.

Faith is the process of learning to accept life as a gift from God.

Beauty Will Save Us

When Jesus described God and God's kingdom, he did so almost always using parables: a hidden treasure found in a field, yeast mixed into a bowl of flour, a sower and seed, a father with a wayward son. "Jesus told the crowds all these things in parables; without a parable he told them nothing" (Matt. 13:34).

Jesus almost never spoke directly but almost always on a slant when he discussed spirituality, because literal language can't transcend into the realm of divinity. The critical thinker wants God to be explained in the reductionist language of instruction manuals and recipe books, but God resides above them in parables and poems.

No one has ever believed that an instruction manual, with its precise language and explicit detail, is a higher piece of literature than *Moby Dick*, *The Odyssey*, or The Chronicles of Narnia, because literal language is the lowest form of communication. Yet repeatedly, we try to drag God down into the world of instruction manuals and step-by-step plans, while God invites us to ascend into a kingdom not of this world.

The slanted truth of the poet, the songwriter, and the storyteller can save us from our cynicism. And it can give CPR to lungs that are full of doubt and breathe life into songless lips by enabling us to see the beauty that's always around. Good art reveals the lies in our perception by blurring our lines of what beauty is supposed to be.

I know this, and I'm not an art expert.

At an early age—eighth grade to be precise—I realized that I was not the most gifted artist. My overly experienced art teacher asked us to raise a hand if we were taking art class the next year in high school. Like an overlooked cornstalk in a harvested field, my minuscule thirteen-year-old arm stood alone in the back of the classroom. Fright filled her octogenarian eyes, and she said in front of all my classmates, "Luke, you shouldn't take art in high school, because you would ruin art class for the rest of the class!"

I took art every year of high school.

But even I, the unwanted eighth-grade artist, know that paint-by-numbers art is the lowest form of art, because where is the creativity and excitement? The best one can do is create a mediocre replica of the picture on the box's cover. If we want a facsimile, we have printers for that.

The beauty of God isn't experienced when we follow a paint-by-numbers God but when we experience the beauty of what God is.

Let go of expectations and experience what is. Cease any attempts to control what divinity is to be and humbly receive what God is. Make peace with the ways boundaries are broken, no matter how painful. Accept how God has disappointed you by not being what you think a good god should be. Then develop a lifestyle of practices that force you into the posture of Jesus toward the world, giving you eyes to see and ears to hear the beauty of God.

Reasoning

Contrary to much of what we think, rarely do any of us reason ourselves into faith; it's the emotional response to beauty that converts us.

When our faith is only logic, we end up like the dumbfounded first-century religious leader Nicodemus, who said to Jesus that he was unable to be reborn because he was too old (and too big) to enter back into his mother's womb. He wanted to drag

God down into the world of instruction manuals, while God was inviting him to ascend into a kingdom not of this world by being born again.

I'm not saying there isn't a place for reason, but I am saying that reason's place is not as big as we think.

The Scottish philosopher David Hume argued that people do not make cold, hard, rational decisions, as Plato claimed. Hume said, "Reason is, and ought only to be the slave of the passions, and can never pretend to any other office than to serve and obey them."[5]

We make emotional decisions and then look for evidence to confirm our already established decisions and we see this philosophical assumption played out not only in theology but also in politics. Modern political theater is our society's Rorschach inkblot test showing everyone what's in our hearts. We vote for or against a candidate and then rarely change our opinion about that candidate regardless of what new revelations surface. Instead, we spin every story to fit our already established perspective. If he or she is our candidate, then the negative report is a lie. If he or she is their candidate, then the positive report is fake news.

University of Virginia psychologist Jonathan Haidt, author of *The Happiness Hypothesis*, built on Hume's argument using the analogy of the president and the press secretary. Our emotions and passions, or as Haidt calls them, the automatic system, are the president making the decisions. Our logic is the press secretary spinning the decisions to make them sound as good as possible, despite not having any involvement in the decision-making process. The press secretary and our logic aren't major decision makers, but they do spend most of the time convincing everyone else of the virtue of the decision.[6]

Most apologetics books are read by people who have already made up their minds about God, whether they can admit it or not. The average apologetics readers are trying to gather as much evidence as possible to support their already reached decision. There is nothing wrong with reading apologetics to confirm our beliefs; it's human nature. But we need to be honest about what's actually going on.

The most meaningful sermons and books don't change how we feel as much as they give us the ability to express the feelings we already have. The sermons we connect to the most aren't those that make us think something we've never thought before but those that say what we've never been able to articulate. Obviously, this is an overgeneralization, but we are generally drawn to content that rationalizes the conclusions we've already reached.

The flip side of Hume's and Haidt's assumptions explains the limitations of apologetics to argue someone into faith. We usually don't reason ourselves into faith. We experience the beauty of God, then we learn to explain it. What we need isn't a better argument but a better appreciation of beauty.

Antoine de Saint-Exupery is believed to have said, "If you want to build a ship, don't drum up people to collect wood and don't assign them tasks and work, but rather teach them to long for the endless immensity of the sea."[7]

We need to spend less time arguing and more time appreciating the beauty and the immensity of the revealed God.

We must not reduce Scripture to our expectations. We must let it be the story of all stories that speaks of love and truth in an ugly world full of lies. We can't reason away the leap. Instead, we need to focus on the beauty that makes us want to take the leap.

Behold beauty, and God's love will be found, because God is love, and beauty is that love manifest.

Greater Things

John's Gospel contains a story about Jesus's disciple Nathanael coming to faith because Jesus was able to tell Nathanael facts about him that appeared to be unknowable. When Jesus said that he saw Nathanael under a tree, Nathanael proclaimed Jesus to be the Son of God and the King of Israel. Jesus responded, "Do you believe because I told you that I saw you under the fig tree? You will see greater things than these" (John 1:50).

What initially spurred Nathanael on to faith was great to get him started, but Jesus knew there would be greater things in store. Like Nathanael, many of us came to faith for reasons that will later be seen as insignificant.

Some of us initially declared our allegiance to Jesus because he lived up to all our expectations.

Maybe we thought that Jesus would make life easy.

Maybe we thought that Jesus would give us the answers that would make sense of all our questions.

Maybe we thought that Jesus would give us a sense of control.

Maybe we came to faith because a youth pastor made us feel really guilty for watching R-rated movies or for making out with a boyfriend and we needed something to get rid of the guilt.

Maybe it was to make a family member happy.

Maybe it was a quest for certainty in a world of confusion.

Maybe it was to assuage our fear of death.

Whatever our reasons for coming to faith back then, maybe they wouldn't motivate us in the same way today.

It might be easy to look down on those reasons now. You might even think you were foolish or gullible to have been motivated by them. Don't do that to yourself. Be grateful for the reasons that got you into the room. You could have ended up in any number of worse rooms. But know that getting in the room is only the beginning.

Don't look down on what got you started. Just don't expect it to be what gets you to the end, because there are greater things to be seen than these.

May you have eyes to see them.

My Prayer for You

If you are struggling to keep your faith afloat, my prayer is for you to have perseverance. Keep daring to spread your arms into the cruciform posture of Jesus no matter how foolish and fruitless it appears.

If you feel disappointed by God, be like Jacob, who didn't let go of God until receiving a blessing.

If you are fighting to make sense of faith, continue to find practices that feed your faith and cease looking for the singular answer that will remove all doubt. Keep trying to trust in God, because even when you are unsure about God, we can see in the life of Jesus that God is sure about you.

Find a community of people who continue to stretch out their arms and continue to have a song to sing.

Find the practices that give life to you and keep the God part of your brain firing.

Trust that eventually you will find the beauty that forms the core, the skeleton, around which you can build your life.

And hopefully, you can join me in singing the song that's on my lips now:

> Who, though he was in the form of God,
>   did not regard equality with God
>   as something to be exploited,
> but emptied himself,
>   taking the form of a slave,
>   being born in human likeness.
> And being found in human form,
>   he humbled himself
>   and became obedient to the point of death—
>   even death on a cross.
> Therefore God also highly exalted him
>   and gave him the name
>   that is above every name,
> so that at the name of Jesus
>   every knee should bend,
>   in heaven and on earth and under the earth,
> and every tongue should confess
>   that Jesus Christ is Lord,
>   to the glory of God the Father. (Phil. 2:6–11)

ACKNOWLEDGMENTS

Avery, Adalyn, and Audrey—I haven't heard the audible sound of the voice of God, but I've heard your giggles filling our house, and that's enough for me. You three are the best thing that ever happened to me, and I've loved every minute of being your father.

Mom and Dad—much love.

Wade Hodges—for showing me the *War of Art*.

Mikel Faulkner—for being a fan of Chet and me.

Paul Nevison—the best indicator for this book's progress was when your feedback went from "I'm proud of you for trying" to "This isn't bad."

Greg Daniel—for showing me the kwan.

Chad Allen, Gisèle Mix, and the rest of the Baker team—I'm beyond grateful for this opportunity and your support.

Jonathan Storment—for always being ready for some awesome.

Moran Church of Christ, Venture Community, and Westover.

Special thanks to my lunch group participants (shout out to Nancy). Remember, you agreed to give me the intellectual ownership of your ideas.

Zane and Marla Busch.

Accountants, avocados, Big Red, Chipotle, Danielle Hejl, D. W. Pierce, Emily Cook, Explosions in the Sky, Halo Top, and sharks.

And most of all to you, Lindsay. The best is yet to come.

NOTES

Chapter 1 Can't Sing

1. 1 Cor. 15:12–19.

Chapter 2 God Equals Good

1. Eugene Peterson, *As Kingfishers Catch Fire* (New York: WaterBrook, 2017), 246.

2. For more on the idea of *deus ex machina* and Dietrich Bonhoeffer's rejection of the *deus ex machina*, see Peter Rollins, *Insurrection* (New York: Howard, 2011).

3. "N. T. Wright: The Day the Revolution Began," *Newsworthy with Norsworthy* (podcast), November 7, 2016, https://lukenorsworthy.com/2016/11/07/n-t-wright-the-day-the-revolution-began/.

4. Wikipedia, s.v. "1755 Lisbon Earthquake," last updated February 2, 2018, https://en.wikipedia.org/wiki/1755_Lisbon_earthquake.

5. Miroslav Volf, *Flourishing: Why We Need Religion in a Globalized World* (New Haven: Yale University Press, 2015), 22.

6. Andrew Newberg and Mark Robert Waldman, *How God Changes Your Brain: Breakthrough Findings from a Leading Neuroscientist* (New York: Ballantine Books, 2010), chap. 1, Kindle. And to be clear, Newberg's claim that God changes the brain isn't a truth claim about the existence of God.

7. Newberg and Waldman, *How God Changes Your Brain*, chap. 1.

8. "Why Do We Say, 'God Bless You,' When Someone Sneezes?," Got Questions, https://www.gotquestions.org/God-bless-you-sneeze .html.

Chapter 3 Binary to Beauty

1. Mark 8:35.

2. 1 Cor. 13:12.

3. Barbara Brown Taylor, *Gospel Medicine* (Boston: Cowley Publications, 1995), 121.

4. C. S. Lewis, *Letters to Malcolm: Chiefly on Prayer* (UK: Harcourt Brace, 1963), 75.

5. Augustine, *Sermons* 241 (Easter ca. 411 AD), http://www.vatican.va /spirit/documents/spirit_20000721_agostino_en.html.

6. This story is told in Peter Enns, *The Sin of Certainty* (San Franscisco: HarperOne, 2016), 178.

7. Joan Chittister, *Between the Dark and the Daylight: Embracing the Contradictions of Life* (New York: Image, 2015), 12.

Chapter 4 Story, Not Answer

1. Regarding Cain and Abel and God not just allowing the conflict but causing the conflict, here is what Old Testament scholar Walter Brueggemann says: "Essential to the plot is the capricious freedom of Yahweh. Like the narrator, we must resist every effort to explain it. There is nothing here of Yahweh preferring cowboys to farmers. There is nothing here to disqualify Cain. . . . The family would perhaps have gotten along better without this God. But he is there. All through the Genesis narratives, Yahweh is there to disrupt, to create tensions, and to evoke the shadowy side of reality." *Genesis: Interpretation Commentary for Teaching and Preaching* (Atlanta: John Knox, 1982), 56–57.

2. Francis Spufford, *Unapologetic* (New York: HarperOne, 2013), 106.

3. Barbara Brown Taylor, *Learning to Walk in the Dark* (New York: HarperOne, 2014).

4. "Barbara Brown Taylor: Learning to Walk in the Dark," *Newsworthy with Norsworthy* (podcast), April 21, 2014, https://lukenorsworthy .com/2014/04/21/barbara-brown-taylor-learning-to-walk-in-the -dark/.

5. Peterson, *As Kingfishers Catch Fire*, 281.

6. Regarding the name Jacob: I know many people have the name Jacob now, and I don't want you to get the wrong impression. I'm not saying you are a bad person. I'm saying your parents thought you were a bad person. My publisher has forced me to say I'm kidding. And that's true.

7. Jason Jones's story is in his book *Limping but Blessed* (Minneapolis: Fortress Press, 2017).

8. Jones, *Limping but Blessed*, 126.

9. Ian Morgan Cron, *Jesus, My Father, and the CIA* (New York: Thomas Nelson, 2011), 172.

10. Cron, *Jesus, My Father, and the CIA*, 175.

11. Warren Buffett, "My Philanthropic Pledge," The Giving Pledge, https://givingpledge.org/Pledger.aspx?id=177.

Chapter 5 Character, Not Container

1. Mark Bowden, *Killing Pablo: The Hunt for the World's Greatest Outlaw* (New York: Atlantic, 2001).

2. Technically speaking, the God of the Bible doesn't send lightning bolts to strike people down. That would be Zeus. But full disclosure: in the Old Testament, God did send bears to kill people, which of the ways to go compared to a lightning bolt might be more unbearable.

3. Richard Rohr, "Incarnation Instead of Atonement," Center for Action and Contemplation, February 12, 2016, https://cac.org/incarnation -instead-of-atonement-2016-02-12/.

4. For more on the John Aldridge story, see Paul Tough, "A Speck in the Sea," *New York Times*, January 5, 2014, https://www.nytimes.com/20 14/01/05/magazine/a-speck-in-the-sea.html.

5. Taylor, *Learning to Walk in the Dark*, 138.

6. Thanks for the help on string theory, Professor Emeritus Ed Holley and Dr. Paul Wallace. While you are at it, read Paul Wallace's book *Stars Beneath Us*.

7. "Newsweek Poll: 90% Believe in God," *Newsweek*, April 8, 2007, http://www.newsweek.com/newsweek-poll-90-believe-god-97611.

8. Alvin Plantinga, *Warranted Christian Belief* (New York: Oxford University Press, 2000), 406.

Chapter 6 Dust and Divine

1. Amos 5:21.

2. Rom. 7:19.

3. "Jason Micheli: Cancer Is Funny," *Newsworthy with Norsworthy* (podcast), January 23, 2017, https://lukenorsworthy.com/2017/01/23/jason-micheli-cancer-is-funny/. Jason Micheli wrote about his cancer diagnosis in *Cancer Is Funny* (Minneapolis: Fortress Press, 2016), which, I must admit, I still haven't read. Sorry, Jason, but I did recommend it to my friend Sally, and she said it was good.

4. I heard this story first from Pete Rollins. His Irish accent makes it sound way cooler, so go back and reread the parable with an Irish accent.

5. Julian, *The Works of the Emperor Julian*, vol. 3, *Letters*, trans. W. C. Wright, Loeb Classical Library (Cambridge, MA: Harvard University Press, 1923), 22.

6. On the benefits of denominations keeping their names, listen to "Jonathan Martin and Ian Morgan Cron," *Newsworthy with Norsworthy* (podcast), June 8, 2015, https://lukenorsworthy.com/2015/06/08/jonathan-martin-and-ian-morgan-cron/.

7. Richard Rohr's book on the two halves of life is *Falling Upward: A Spirituality for the Two Halves of Life* (San Francisco: Jossey-Bass, 2011).

A Biblical Interlude

1. Heb. 4:12.

2. Terrance F. Ross, "Welcome to Smarter Basketball," *Atlantic*, June 25, 2015, https://www.theatlantic.com/entertainment/archive/2015/06/nba-data-analytics/396776/.

3. Ross, "Welcome to Smarter Basketball."

4. Michael Lewis, "The No-Stats All-Star," *New York Times Magazine*, February 13, 2009, http://www.nytimes.com/2009/02/15/maga zine/15Battier-t.html. For more on analytics in sports, read Michael Lewis's outstanding book *TheUndoing Project*.

5. "Steve Nash on Lost Titles, Modern Point Guards, and Soccer Superstars (Ep. 194)," Soundcloud, *The Bill Simmons Podcast*, March 29, 2017, 55:00, https://soundcloud.com/the-bill-simmons-pod cast/steve-nash-on-lost-titles-modern-point-guards-and-soccer-super stars-ep-194.

6. Kalyn Kahler, "Andrew Hawkins: Just as Smart as I Am Quick," *Sports Illustrated*, May 19, 2017, https://www.si.com/mmqb/2017/05/19 /nfl-andrew-hawkins-columbia-university-graduation.

7. Thomas Albright and Jed Rakoff, "Eyewitnesses Aren't as Reliable as You Might Think," *Washington Post*, January 30, 2015, https://www .washingtonpost.com/opinions/eyewitnesses-arent-as-reliable-as-you -might-think/2015/01/30/fe1bc26c-7a74-11e4-9a27-6fdbc612bf f8_story.html.

Chapter 7 Bounding, Not Boxing

1. "Newsweek Poll: 90% Believe in God."

2. John Bingham, "Richard Dawkins: I Can't Be Sure God Does Not Exist," *Telegraph*, February 24, 2012, http://www.telegraph.co.uk/news /religion/9102740/Richard-Dawkins-I-cant-be-sure-God-does-not -exist.html.

3. Jimmy Fallon, *The Tonight Show*, April 5, 2015, https://www.facebook .com/FallonTonight/photos/a.443222478895.217143.317324838 95/10153220637823896/?type=3&theater.

4. "A parallel of sorts is provided by the Fourth Gospel, where believing is always a verb, never a noun; faith is not a possession but an activity. It is like a song that disappears when we stop singing." Douglas Hare, *Matthew: Interpretation Commentary for Teaching and Preaching* (Atlanta: John Knox, 1993), 170. For more on faith as a way of life, not a set of beliefs, see Enns, *Sin of Certainty*.

5. Larry Hurtado, *Destroyer of the Gods* (Waco: Baylor University Press, 2017), chap. 2, Kindle.

6. Despite the bad reputation Thomas earned by his doubting, we shouldn't forget that in John 11:16 he courageously volunteered to go and die.

7. Richard Rohr, *Everything Belongs: The Gift of Contemplative Prayer* (New York: Crossroad, 2003), 53.

8. Matt Jenson, *The Gravity of Sin: Augustine, Luther, and Barth on "homo incurvatus in se"* (New York: T&T Clark, 2006).

9. Matt. 12:38–40; 16:1–4.

10. T. S. Eliot, *Murder in the Cathedral* (NY: Harcourt, Brace, 1935), 44.

11. The importance of silence for preacher/teacher types was first conveyed to me by Mike McHargue, author of *Finding God in the Waves*.

12. Thomas Merton, *No Man Is an Island* (Boston: Shambhala, 2005), 134.

Chapter 8 God over god

1. M. Scott Peck, *The Road Less Traveled* (New York: Simon & Schuster, 1978), 88.

2. Stanley Hauerwas, "Sex and Politics: Bertrand Russell and 'Human Sexuality,'" *Christian Century*, April 19, 1978, 417–22.

3. Phil. 3:13–14.

4. "Maya Angelou: I'm Trying to Be a Christian," *Telegraph*, May 29, 2014, http://www.telegraph.co.uk/culture/culturevideo/108619 20/Maya-Angelou-Im-trying-to-be-a-Christian.html.

5. Quoted in Jonathan Haidt, *The Happiness Hypothesis: Finding Modern Truth in Ancient Wisdom* (New York: Basic Books, 2006), 17.

6. "Jonathan Haidt," interview by Tamler Sommers, *Believer*, August 2005, https://www.believermag.com/issues/200508/?read=interview _haidt.

7. The quote seems to be a generous translation attributed to Antoine de Saint-Exupery. See his book *The Wisdom of the Sands* [*Citadelle*], trans. Stuart Gilbert (Chicago: University of Chicago Press, 1984).

Luke Norsworthy is the senior minister of Westover Hills Church of Christ and hosts the *Newsworthy with Norsworthy* podcast. He and his wife, Lindsay, and their three daughters, Avery, Adalyn, and Audrey, live in Austin, Texas.

Get connected with
LUKE!

Listen to Luke's podcast
Newsworthy with Norsworthy
at **LukeNorsworthy.com**

 NewsworthywithNorsworthy | Lukenors | LukeNorsworthy